W9-ARG-846

the series on school reform

Ann Lieberman, *Senior Scholar, Stanford University*   Joseph P. McDonald, *New York University*
SERIES EDITORS

(Continued)

the series on school reform, *continued*

Failing at School

Lessons for Redesigning Urban High Schools

Camille A. Farrington

TEACHERS COLLEGE PRESS

Teachers College, Columbia University
New York and London

KH

Published by Teachers College Press, 1234 Amsterdam Avenue, New York, NY 10027

Library of Congress Cataloging-in-Publication Data available at www.loc.gov.

ISBN 978-0-8077-5516-7 (paper)
eISBN 978-0-8077-7274-4 (ebook)

Printed on acid-free paper
Manufactured in the United States of America

21 20 19 18 17 16 15 14   8 7 6 5 4 3 2 1

8/12/15

Contents

Series Foreword

For several decades, the Series on School Reform has published books that relate to improving schools for students and their teachers. Lest one thinks that school reform is a one-time thing, look at the books in this series over time as they reveal the complexities, strategies, and possibilities for school reform. Two reform perspectives have emerged. One is that reforms can be mandated, assuming that teachers and students will conform to the new ideas and the problem is poor teachers, while another is that school reform can only really change the way students learn and teachers teach by involving all members of the school community in changing the way things are done. Each of these perspectives has generated different forms of reform. This series represents knowledge and practices from the latter of these perspectives.

Five big themes have been written about in this series: *leadership* at all levels of the system, *teachers* and their centrality in reform efforts, *students* and ways to involve them, different ways to think about building *communities* in and across schools, and *networks and partnerships* as different ways to organize for improvement.

The series has attempted to get at the complexities of all these themes, encouraging research and practice to elevate our knowledge, as well as the practices that are created to generate constructive changes in school systems. As is evident from all the books in the series and as Seymour Sarason said years ago, "One thing you know is that there will always be problems when you try to change anything." The School Reform Series shows that his comment was right on target. What we learn from all these studies, projects, and descriptions of change is that the processes of change and the organizational arrangements, as well as new and creative ideas, are what we continue to learn as different members of the school community engage in school improvements of all kinds. All of these changes include challenges as well as improvements.

Charter schools and performance assessments as well as the creation of the Common Core State Standards are the latest reform ideas. They, too, involve changes in the state and local requirements of schools on the one hand, and a different way of teaching and assessing learning on the other. These ideas, like the many before them, will demand new ways of thinking about professional development, building the capacity of teachers, principals, and district personnel as well as changes in how we assess learning.

The School Reform Series will continue to find ways that people write about the current reforms and how they are being enacted, their possibilities, their problems, and their perplexities through important research, practice, and policies.

—Ann Lieberman, senior scholar, Stanford University

Preface

"What if the secret to success is failure?" asks journalist Paul Tough in his book *How Children Succeed*. A parenting website called *The Capables* promotes a similar idea: "We need to get excited about the possibility of our children failing, because if they are not failing, they are not risking greatness." J. K. Rowling, Michael Jordan, Albert Einstein, and Thomas Edison have all pointed to failure as essential to their prodigious success. Their message seems particularly salient for those of us raising children. If we coddle our kids and shield them from failure, how will they learn to handle setbacks? Develop grit and determination? Discover their inner potential? "And yet we know," wrote Tough, "that what kids need more than anything is a little hardship: some challenge, some deprivation that they can overcome, even if just to prove to themselves that they can" (p. 84).

But what if failure can't be overcome? I have spent the past 20-plus years in and around urban public high schools. In this context, I'd propose that kids don't have a shortage of challenge, deprivation, or character-building opportunities to fail. Instead, I see young people awash in failure that does not serve them, set within an outdated system that makes it nearly impossible for them to benefit from their mistakes or regain their footing once they start to fall. Failure as we currently have it structured does not meet the academic, developmental, or motivational needs of adolescents. Most important, academic failure leads almost inevitably to bad long-term outcomes, most notably to dropping out of school. Rather than building students' character, motivating them to persevere, or allowing them to reach their full potential, academic failure may well be ruining their lives.

This book examines failure in the American public high school and argues that we cannot significantly reduce its occurrence or the harm it causes unless we remake the system that gives rise to it. To do so, *we* must learn from failure—the failure of our current system to adequately prepare young people for the future. We have to understand the history of failure in secondary education and the structures, policies, practices, and beliefs that perpetuate it in our own high schools every day.

My interests in this topic are both professional and personal. As a former high school teacher, I have watched too many teenagers slide down the slippery slope of academic failure and drop out of sight. After 15 years of teaching, I left the classroom and re-entered academia to study the roots of high school failure and to explore how it might be interrupted. This book draws upon my subsequent research, the work of my colleagues, and a broad base of empirical and practice evidence to lay out a framework for thinking about the problems with our current secondary education institutions and to suggest a different path forward.

Acknowledgments

Over the past 25 years, my colleagues, students, mentors, family, and friends have shaped my understanding of adolescents and American high schools, giving rise to an alternative vision for the relationship between the two. I will be forever indebted to Dr. Margaret Small, Mary Ann Pitcher, and the extraordinary faculty, students, and staff at a once-upon-a-time Chicago charter school. You are etched forever in my heart and shape every thought I think. Margaret particularly influenced my understanding of how structural problems in high schools contribute to educational inequalities.

At Skyline High School in Oakland, California, and Oregon High School in Oregon, Wisconsin—two entirely different places (and not the schools I write about in this book)—I learned from dedicated co-workers who loved teenagers and worked tirelessly to create educational environments that not only prepared students academically, but instilled in them a love of history, literature, music, and a sense of themselves as creative people venturing into an interesting world. My eternal respect and gratitude go to those who wake up every morning and head to a high school classroom.

I have been blessed by the wisdom and generosity of excellent mentors and teachers, most particularly Anna Richert at Mills College, who sent me into the teaching profession in 1991 as an agent of change; and Mark Smylie, Carol Myford, David Mayrowetz, Rebekah Levin, John D'Emilio, and Dionne Danns at the University of Illinois at Chicago, who taught me how to do much of what I did in this book.

At The University of Chicago, enormous thanks for the ongoing support and intellectual community created by my extraordinary ally, friend, and mentor Melissa Roderick; to my collaborator and thought partner Jenny Nagaoka; to the world's best research and practice team of Nicole Beechum, Tasha Seneca Keyes, Faye Kroshinsky, David Johnson, Rachel Levenstein, Shanette Porter, Ann Szekely, Courtney Thompson, Matt Holsapple, Thomas Kelley-Kemple, Eliza Moeller, Billie Jo Day, and Kersti Azar at the School of Social Service Administration; to Elaine Allensworth and colleagues at the Consortium on Chicago School Research for their inspiring work; and to the righteous education visionaries at the Network for College Success: Mary Ann Pitcher, Sarah Howard, Sarah Duncan, Jackie Lemon, Amy Torres, Adelric McCain, Liz Monge Pacheco, Yolanda Knight, Krystal Muldrow, Julie Price Daly, Julie Barnes, Sandra Ortigoza, Meghan Bauer, LaKisha

Pittman, Cecily Langford, and the School Improvement Grant (SIG) teams across Chicago public high schools. I am inspired every day by your passion, intelligence, and commitment to the students, teachers, and school leaders in the Chicago Public Schools. I also extend heartfelt thanks to my former colleagues at the University of Washington, particularly Mike Knapp for encouraging me to write this book and my dear friend Margery Ginsberg for unfailing support, camaraderie, and a sense of humor throughout. I am grateful for Pat Wasley's early support for this project.

Many people gave thoughtful feedback on this manuscript. A huge thank you to my former student Molly Backes and her fellow Grinnell alum Cameron Gale for their thorough reading and excellent suggestions. I am indebted to Nate Okpych, Bronwyn McDaniel, Tasha Seneca Keyes, Emily Krone, Margery Ginsberg, Jenny Nagaoka, Melissa Roderick, Mark Smylie, and Ken Rasinski for making this book better. The Coalition of Essential Schools supported my dissertation research with a Theodore R. Sizer Fellowship, for which I am most grateful.

A special word of thanks is due to Marie Ellen Larcada, my editor at Teachers College Press, for her patience and encouragement over 4 years. Let's just say that if she had a strict "No Late Work" policy, I would have failed for sure. Thank you for caring about the end product more than the deadlines. Here's hoping that someday teachers across America will routinely extend the same courtesy to their students.

To my beautiful daughters, Tenaya and Tessa, I love you for bearing with me through several years of divided attention as I worked on this book, and I thank you for your help in editing and reference-checking along the way. Most important, you gave me an understanding of teenagers and high school I could never have gleaned from teaching, researching, or reading, and you make my life joyful beyond measure. To my husband, Mark Courtney, you make this all possible in every way, every day. Words cannot express my deep love and gratitude.

Finally, my heartfelt thanks to the students, teachers, and administrators at the schools I refer to here as Devon, Alexander, and Maxwell High Schools for letting me into your lives and trusting me with your stories. I hope I have done justice to your struggles, and that your words move mountains.

Failing at School

Lessons for Redesigning Urban High Schools

Part I

REFLECTING

Whenever you find yourself on the side of the majority, it is time to pause and reflect.

—Mark Twain

Introduction

Failure in Urban American High Schools

Every day, teenagers fail in public educational institutions meant to prepare them for meaningful participation in the adult world. For the most part, these kids keep showing up to school for years after receiving those first Fs, trying to get an education. But most adolescents who fail courses in 9th grade don't ever stop failing, regardless of how much they try. Surprisingly few ever regain their footing to graduate. I argue in these pages that so many students fail out of school not because of their own flawed characters or intellectual inadequacies, but because high schools were designed in a way that produces widespread failure. Unless we change the system, kids will continue to fail and drop out in large numbers.

The scale of urban high school failure is unconscionable. When producers at Chicago Public Radio station WBEZ reported on the city's dropout problem in 2009, they called the series "*50/50*" because those were the rough odds that a student entering a Chicago public high school would actually earn a diploma. On average, across most large U.S. cities, only about 6 in 10 entering freshmen make it to graduation (Swanson, 2010). That means roughly 40% of students in our nation's large cities leave school without any credentials and without the skills or knowledge necessary for productive employment.

The public high school is our institution, and hence its failure is our failure. Imagine a roller coaster that pulls away from the loading platform with its cars filled but returns each time half-empty, former passengers strewn across the landscape. The amusement park operators just keep shaking their heads and reloading the cars with new riders: "We always say to hold on, but some people just don't listen." As a country, and most particularly as educators, administrators, and policymakers, we are at the controls yet we aren't taking responsibility for the ones we cast off. We systematically lose almost half the students who start high school under our care and we keep blaming it on the kids, their parents, their neighborhoods, or some larger social forces.

Ultimately, it is we who have failed to devise an effective secondary education system and we who have not been learning our lessons. Rather than continuing to do the same thing and expecting different results—to send the next cohort of students off on that roller-coaster ride and hope for more favorable outcomes—it is time we draw another set of conclusions from high school failure and figure out how to do something radically different.

This book is written for teachers, school leaders, district administrators, educational policymakers, funders, reform advocates, academics, parents, public officials—anyone who cares about young people and worries about high schools, particularly those serving our most vulnerable children in large cities. The chapters that follow lead the reader step by step through a process of reflecting and rethinking—learning from our collective failure—so we can regroup and try something new. My ultimate goal is to offer a blueprint and a set of principles for redesigning the American high school.

Of course, we can't think about high school redesign without wading into the middle of a century-old controversy about the goals of public secondary education (Cuban & Shipps, 2000; Labaree, 1997; Reese, 1995, 2005). Is the purpose of the public high school to provide a rigorous academic education that prepares the most capable students for college? To train youth for their slot in a stratified labor market? To create citizens capable of responsible participation in democratic society? To enable those most disadvantaged by hierarchical social structures of race, class, or language to transcend those barriers? Which purpose(s) should high schools try to serve, and to what extent might these varying purposes require high schools to enact different kinds of structures, policies, and practices—in fact, to be fundamentally different kinds of institutions? What do we want to redesign the American high school to accomplish?

I assert that high school's primary purpose should be to prepare our children to engage productively in the world, to lead fulfilling lives, and to contribute to the greater good. High schools are pivotally important social institutions, particularly in urban districts serving disenfranchised, low-income communities. Urban public high schools are often the last best chance for youth living in poverty to gain a foothold in their entrance to adulthood. Young people in these communities often have no safety nets if their schools fail them.

Unfortunately, on the whole, urban high schools are not very good at preparing adolescents to engage productively in the world, to live fulfilling lives, or to contribute to the greater good. Instead, young people too often leave high school more disengaged and disaffected than they entered, with few skills and little academic knowledge to parlay into a meaningful livelihood. Urban high schools do not necessarily *cause* the problems that derail students, but far too many unwittingly exacerbate the challenges of growing up in troubled communities and offer few real alternatives to the constrained lives many young people know. As a result, a substantial proportion of low-income and racial/ethnic minority youth in cities across this country leave high school with little likelihood of ever reaching their potential. Not only is this morally reprehensible, it is also ill-advised in an increasingly competitive global economy. Wasting human resources does not make for a sustainable society, nor does it bode well for the quality of life of our families, friends, neighbors, co-workers, and fellow citizens.

High schools play a key role in our ability to turn this around. We need to stop, reflect, and learn from our collective institutional failure in American high schools—and then try a different approach.

FOURTEEN STUDENTS NEGOTIATING FAILURE

Failure seems to follow predictable patterns in urban high schools. A student's likelihood of failing a class—relatively uncommon in lower grades—jumps substantially upon entrance to 9th grade. About half the freshmen in a typical urban high school will fail at least one class. Freshmen who fail more than one class are unlikely to ever recover. In Chicago, for instance, only 22% of students who failed two or more semester courses in 9th grade were able to graduate in 4 years (Allensworth & Easton, 2007). In cities across the country, we see a tight connection between freshman course failure and eventual dropout. This leads to exceptionally low rates of high school completion nationally, particularly in racial/ethnic minority communities. In a nation where free K–12 public education is guaranteed, in an economy where a high school education is essential, and in light of studies showing that over 90% of all American youth aspire to go to college, how can it possibly be the case that Black and Latino children in urban districts still have little better than a 50/50 chance of graduating from high school?

To bring to life the common trajectory of failure, this book draws from stories of 14 teenagers attending three public high schools in Chicago. Chicago is the country's third-largest school district and is home to the University of Chicago's Consortium on Chicago School Research (CCSR). CCSR has a repository of over 20 years of extensive data on students and teachers in the Chicago Public Schools and has conducted groundbreaking studies of urban high schools attempting to reform. As such, Chicago makes a great place to study students' high school experience.

Each of the students featured in these pages entered 9th grade with hopes and dreams for the future. They valued education and expected to graduate. Far from the stereotype of uncaring and disaffected urban youth, they saw themselves as competent people with something to offer the world. Most of these students had never failed a class before 9th grade. When they got that first F on their report cards, many of them were shocked. Some were angry. All were disappointed and embarrassed. Eventually, they each picked themselves up and tried again. They followed the pathways laid out by their schools for recovering the course credits they needed to catch up. But despite their efforts, like hundreds of thousands of their peers nationally, most students attending the two conventional high schools in my study fell further and further behind over time.

While these students' stories document the mechanisms of systematic failure, they also collectively highlight another conclusion: Schools can also construct success for struggling students. One of the schools I studied reframed the notion of failure by using a competency-based system for awarding grades and course credits. This alternative approach provides an example of how schools might create pathways to help struggling students recover from early failure, build skills, and graduate. I place the stories of eight students in this innovative school side-by-side with the stories of youth in the two more traditional schools, revealing how many taken-for-granted aspects of high school may in fact be at the heart of widespread academic failure—and what we might do to change that.

SELECTION AND STRATIFICATION OR EQUITY AND EXCELLENCE?

Throughout these chapters, I argue that high school structures, policies, and practices can be sorted into two mutually exclusive categories: those that work to promote *selection and stratification* and those that work to promote *equity and excellence*. These two categories map onto two fundamental functions the American high school has historically been asked to fulfill, even though these functions themselves are contradictory at their heart and logically require two very different sets of structures, policies, and practices.

The *selection and stratification function* holds that the purpose of high schools is to determine the proper place for every student in the existing hierarchical social and economic order and to differentiate curriculum, instruction, support, and opportunity according to each student's expected position. Thus, one child is prepared to enter medical school, while another is prepared to file medical records. "Excellence" is only the goal for the most capable.

In direct contrast, the *equity and excellence function* holds that all students who attend public high school—regardless of race, class, gender, nationality, language, social position, or disability—should receive the same high-quality academic education. Though existing social inequalities are recognized as potential *obstacles* in meeting this goal, proponents of equity and excellence would argue for putting in place structures or supports to ensure that everybody is equally well prepared for the same wide array of postsecondary options. This is not to say that we wouldn't still have surgeons and medical assistants, but rather that all students would leave high school on equal footing to pursue any career or educational path they wanted to pursue. We wouldn't have decided that for them before they were old enough to decide for themselves.

At the bottom line, proponents of selection and stratification accept as given the existing social and economic order and seek to efficiently prepare young people for their designated place within it, where proponents of equity and excellence challenge that order by enabling young people—through education—to transcend the place assigned to them by birth.

Throughout the history of the American high school, the pendulum has swung back and forth as policies were put in place to advance one goal or the other. The legacy of this historical push-pull is that virtually every school policy or practice—and by extension every act of educators, administrators, and policymakers—serves *either* a selection and stratification end *or* an equity and excellence end. This is not to suggest that adults sometimes act maliciously or with intent to limit young people's opportunities. On the contrary, the vast majority of educators I know work hard in what they believe to be the best interests of their students. But sometimes the most well-intentioned professionals engaged in the most routine aspects of schooling still end up adversely affecting students' long-term outcomes.

In my research, I have been particularly interested in this question of how student failure either advances a selection and stratification function or an equity and excellence function. I am operating from the premise that student failure can serve different purposes in different settings, depending on the way an organization structures and responds to it. Within a given school, does failure limit opportunity or mobilize support?

In some educational contexts, student failure may in fact be integral to achieving an organization's mission. The U.S. Air Force's elite pilot training program has a high failure rate: Over the course of rigorous training and examinations, many hopeful applicants can't meet the performance goals and thus fail to make the cut to become a pilot. Failure in this context serves an appropriate selection and stratification function. By screening out less qualified candidates, failure functions to ensure tight quality control in the caliber of American pilots.

Conversely, the recreational youth basketball program at a community park does not try to weed out its least experienced or least talented players as failures, because it has a different orientation and purpose than does the Air Force Academy. Certainly, some young basketball players won't be able to dribble well or sink baskets, but the park district would be unlikely to use the word *failure* to describe kids' subpar athletic performance on the ball court. The goal of the youth basketball program is not to identify top players and weed out poor ones, but to involve all players in the game and help each one develop skills, while reinforcing important concepts such as teamwork. Where failure functions to *limit opportunities* for failing pilots in the Air Force Academy, it most likely functions to *mobilize support* for failing players in the recreational basketball program.

Unfortunately, high schools operate much more like the Air Force Academy than like the park district. Illuminating how school policies and practices structure failure, how failure functions within a given school, and how the function of failure influences the experiences and school trajectories of failing students is a central goal of this book.

ORGANIZATION OF THE CHAPTERS

Failure implies that our performance fell short of some mark, that we did not fulfill something required or expected. Whether failure is personal, collective, or institutional, learning from failure requires that we reflect on our shortfalls in the past, face difficult truths in the present, and champion new possibilities for the future. Thus, the pages that follow are organized in three main Parts: *Reflecting*, *Studying Failure*, and *Going Forward*. We start the process for learning from failure by *Reflecting*.

Step 1 is knowing what we are trying to accomplish and acknowledging the difference between what has been happening and the goal we are pursuing. In light of high school's overarching goal of preparing adolescents for successful futures, Chapter 1—"What We See Versus What We Seek"—examines the current state of our failure to reach this goal from two different angles. The chapter opens with Monique, a Chicago student in the midst of struggling with high school course failure. (All names of students, teachers, administrators, and schools are pseudonyms.) Monique's story is followed by statistics showing the prevalence of different links in the chain of failure in urban American high schools nationally: failed courses, credit deficiency, grade retention, and dropout. Ninth-grade course failure appears to be the first domino in a long and destructive chain of events. I place particular emphasis on understanding why that domino has such devastating momentum.

The second step in learning from failure is reflecting on the path that led us here, finding the patterns, and acknowledging the outcomes of our past attempts. Thus, Chapter 2—"How We Got Here"—takes a historical perspective, arguing not only that the history of American secondary education has always been rife with widespread failure, but also that failure served a very intentional selection and stratification function: Colleges wanted to identify top achievers, and taxpayers didn't want to foot the bill for those at the bottom. High schools were structured to differentiate between young people at different levels of achievement, and failure was used to cull out students on the low end. Chapter 2 also examines the ideological underpinnings of widespread failure, built on old ideas about merit, intelligence, character, and deservingness. I argue that the structures put in place to serve a selection and stratification function in the late 19th century are still alive and well today—and operating as originally intended—regardless of how our goals, needs, and intentions may have changed.

The third step in learning from failure is to draw upon available information and seek out new perspectives to help us think about our present dilemma. To this end, Chapter 3—"What We Now Know About Learning"—summarizes advances in cognitive science and psychological research that shed light on human motivation to learn and the role of psychosocial attitudes and beliefs in school performance. From this perspective, what looked like meritorious individual traits by the rationale reviewed in Chapter 2 start looking like socially constructed advantages in Chapter 3.

Part II—*Studying Failure*—presents the stories of 14 students to widen our perspective on the contemporary mechanisms of failure. Here, we take a close look at how failure plays out in schools and classrooms and what it means in young people's lives. Chapter 4 describes two qualitative studies of students grappling with failure and includes a brief profile of the three Chicago high schools they attended.

Chapters 5, 6, 7, and 8 present data collected from interviews with students, teachers, and administrators from my two studies. Chapter 5 looks at students' explanations for and responses to their first experiences of failure. In many ways, students in the three schools sound remarkably similar here. Once they start talking about grading and credits, however, clear differences emerge. Chapter 6 compares students' experiences with traditional and competency-based grading systems and looks at the effects of each on students' efforts to pass classes. In Chapter 7, we see different ways schools structured opportunities for remediation and credit recovery. We hear students in two traditional high schools grow increasingly frustrated as they fall further behind, while students in a school with a competency-based grading and credit system express confidence that their school has made it possible for them to recover credits and graduate. In Chapter 8, students from all three schools describe teaching practices that support their feelings of competence and success.

Going Forward, the third and final part of the book, takes the last, critical step in our process of learning from failure: devising a new strategy for high school redesign. Chapter 9—"Motivation, Capacity, Competence, Opportunity"—is integrative, pulling together history, ideology, psychology, and empirical research to point to a new vision for American public high schools. If we want secondary education to prepare young people to engage fully and productively in the world, we need to climb out of our well-worn ruts and redesign high schools to achieve those outcomes.

URBAN HIGH SCHOOLS, A CHANGING ECONOMY, AND THE CHALLENGE OF THE COMMON CORE

Modern-day advocates for equity and excellence have argued persuasively for shared national educational standards to ensure that students from all areas of the country and all socioeconomic strata are equally well prepared for college and career. The Common Core State Standards Initiative, a state-led effort, has resulted in the adoption of a shared set of educational standards in mathematics and English language arts for students from kindergarten to grade 12. As of 2013, the Common Core Standards had been adopted by 45 states, the District of Columbia, and four U.S. territories. This is an unprecedented accomplishment and a striking example of a policy focused on equity and excellence.

That being said, we also must acknowledge that the implementation of the Common Core puts us at the brink of both huge opportunity and huge risk. Recent analyses confirm what urban educators have already anticipated: The academic performance of students in most urban high schools today falls far short of what is articulated in the Common Core State Standards. Indeed, judging by the poor performance of urban schools on the generally less rigorous state standards that the Common Core will replace, one might find little reason to be hopeful. To meet the goal of equity and excellence that underlies the Common Core Standards Initiative, urban schools have to figure out how to support students across race and class to meet these new, substantially more challenging academic standards in significant numbers. If we fail to do this, we will see the Common Core become just another mechanism of selection and stratification, advancing and rewarding top performers while setting impossibly high hurdles for everybody else and weeding out a new, record number of failures.

I argue that high schools were originally designed to deliver advanced education only to the most deserving, and that widespread failure was part and parcel of this process. Let me be clear, however, that this design served the United States very well for a long time.

In fact, the American high school through much of the 20th century is one of the world's greatest educational success stories. Think about it. Only 200,000 students attended public high schools in the United States in 1890; by 1920 that number had grown tenfold to more than 2.2 million (Fenske, 1997). By 1940, half of American adolescents finished high school, and by 1969 the proportion was at 77% (Swanson, 2010). Burgeoning participation in secondary education made the American people "the most educated in the world . . . in the century in which education would critically matter," creating a broad middle class and fueling 70 years of economic growth and declining inequality (Goldin & Katz, 2008, p. 2). Though high schools churned out dropouts along with graduates, our strong manufacturing economy meant there were good jobs for dropouts, too.

But beginning around 1970, the world changed substantially, and the old system stopped working. Low-skilled manufacturing jobs began disappearing. The growth in educational attainment slowed sharply, reducing the supply of educated American workers. Earnings have stagnated among lower-wage workers while payoffs to higher education continue to increase, widening gaps between the educated haves and the low-skilled have-nots. Harvard economists Claudia Goldin and Lawrence Katz (2008, 2009) have described these phenomena in studying America's rising income inequality, and they make this pointed observation:

> One important factor [in rising inequality] . . . is the stagnation of secondary-school graduation rates and the fact that too many high school graduates are inadequately prepared to pass college courses. Not so long ago, the American economy grew rapidly and wages grew in tandem, with education playing a large, positive role in both. The United States led the way in mass education and was, until fairly recently, many decades ahead of even the rich nations of Europe. The challenge now is to revitalize education-based mobility. For without it, it appears that the technological advances that largely drive economic growth will increasingly divide the nation. (2009, p. 33)

In the early 21st century, low-income and racial/ethnic minority students have no real economic alternatives to educational attainment. The American urban high school must figure out a way to ensure that students succeed amid the challenging context of the Common Core State Standards, graduate from high school, and are well prepared for college. There can be no equity and excellence without meeting this goal.

The good news is that we have very clear models of how we might redesign high schools to reduce the traditional casualties of failure and better prepare our youth for the demands of the 21st century. But first we must acknowledge that what we have been doing no longer works. We need to reflect on our failures, review what we know, and dedicate ourselves to creating the kind of high schools that can take us where we want to go.

If the purpose of American secondary education is to separate the wheat from the chaff, and if we as a nation can live with the reality that wealthier and Whiter youth will always be the wheat and low-income and minority youth will always be the chaff, then we ought to keep high schools exactly as they are. They are doing a bang-up job of perpetuating this. If, however, we believe that every child in America ought to reap the benefits of a quality K–12 education and have realistic access to college, that children of every race and class ought to be able to make for themselves a decent life, to earn for themselves a family-supporting wage, and to participate fully in the civic life of our democracy, then we need to ensure that America's public high schools are designed to realize those visions. By better understanding the ways our current psychological assumptions and institutional structures contribute to high failure and dropout rates for low-income and minority students, we will be better able to transform urban high schools into places where young people can learn from any missteps, recover from their failures, and graduate to become fully productive and engaged citizens—the kinds of people the world desperately needs to solve the daunting challenges before us.

ONE

What We See Versus What We Seek

Faces of Failure in Urban High Schools

Failure has many faces in urban high schools. One of those faces belongs to Monique. I met Monique in spring of 2008. She was 15, an African American girl with a good heart and sense of humor, being raised by elderly grandparents after the death of her mom. She attended a Chicago public high school in a poor, distressed neighborhood. In spring of sophomore year, I asked Monique about her life, her dreams, and her experiences of school.

FAILING MONIQUE

Looking back on her days in elementary school, Monique had to admit she was maybe "a little wild." She liked classes when she understood what the teacher was talking about, "but then it's like, when it get hard in there, some of the work that I can't do, then no, I don't like it." Her grades were mostly Cs and a few Ds before entering Alexander High School in 2006. Compared to elementary school, which Monique described as a supportive environment, 9th grade suddenly felt like "you are on your own." Teachers had too many students, she explained, to take time for each one.

Every morning Monique woke up at 6:00, got dressed, and helped prepare breakfast for her family before catching the bus to school. Along with two younger siblings, she had lived with her grandparents for much of her life because, as she described it, "my mother never had time for me." She met her father only once as a child, a chance encounter on the street. When Monique was in 5th grade her mother died, and her only caretakers were elderly and frail, in need of care themselves. One afternoon in the middle of an interview, Monique pulled from her purse a carefully kept 5 x 7 photograph of her mother at about age 18, a pretty and well-coiffed young woman smiling proudly in a blue graduation gown. I found it poignant that Monique carried around that picture as she struggled to earn her own high school diploma.

Monique knew she needed a good education. Her expectations were "for me to do my best and graduate." She hoped to go to college, maybe become "an RN nurse." She told me the difference between students who drop out of school and students who work hard and graduate is that the latter are the kind of people who say, "Hey, I want something in life." Monique counted herself among those who wanted something.

Despite the value she placed on education, Monique had a mixed academic record by the end of 9th grade. She finished the year with just over a C average (2.3 GPA), but she failed algebra, literature, and one semester of science. She started 10th grade with 5 course credits toward the 24 she would need to graduate, slightly behind her peers. This put Monique on a slippery slope that would characterize the rest of her high school experience, as she played "catch up" to get back on track toward graduation. She retook one semester of algebra in night school, eventually earning another half-credit. Tenth grade started well; she was only failing gym on her November report card. But as sophomore year progressed, Monique found school too "boring" and was frequently late, often missing morning classes. As her absences accumulated, so did her failing grades.

Outside of school Monique was enmeshed in an emotionally draining court battle that dragged on through much of sophomore year. (She had been the victim of a traumatic assault.) At 15, she was responsible for cooking and caring for her disabled grandparents and younger brother and sister, often making her tardy to school. She struggled to keep up in her classes while also attending evening algebra class in another part of town. I made the comment to Monique that she had a lot of responsibilities. "Too much for a teenager," she replied.

This all took its toll on Monique's academic work. On most school days, she confessed, "I could not concentrate, period." As her frustration mounted, Monique started acting out and getting suspended. She was absent 35 days in spring semester, many due to suspensions for disciplinary infractions. By late May of sophomore year, Monique was missing quite a few assignments. Teachers' policies on late work were going to make it impossible for her to earn enough points to pass most of her classes, even if she managed to turn in all her missing work. Her third-quarter report card had two Ds, four Fs and one A (in choir). She told me she loved music, but other classes "feel boring when you don't know what they talking about 'cause you wasn't here." Monique knew she would likely end the semester earning no additional credits, save for music, putting her even further behind her classmates.

The vast majority of adults at Alexander High School were caring, dedicated educators who worked hard to help students succeed. The school implemented a daily advisory period to build relationships between students and staff members and to provide support, advice, and assistance in navigating high school. Monique was put in a special advisory due to her missing credits, but she felt like no one paid attention to her there. She was lost in her classes and felt as though few teachers reached out to help. She dutifully attended night school to make up her algebra credit, but the late hours and extra work undermined her ability to keep up in daytime classes.

Although Alexander High School did not cause Monique's problems, neither did it adequately address them or support her to succeed despite them. The last time I saw Monique, she was resigned to attending summer school and then another stint at night school the following year. She looked forward to turning things around: "My junior year, I'm gonna be on it. I'm not playing no games. No missing days, period. Doing my work." I asked why she persisted even when her chances of graduation looked increasingly slim. She looked up and said, "'Cause I know that school is something that I need in life." When I checked on her progress a few months later, I learned Monique had been dropped from the summer school roster for excessive absences. As she entered her third year of high school, she still had only 5.5 credits toward the 24 required for graduation.

Monique was born to a single mother with little money and apparently little else to offer her daughter, but Monique should not be doomed to a life of poverty and strife. Once her grandparents are gone, I wonder how she would support herself and her brother and sister without a high school diploma. Public education could have made a positive difference in Monique's life; she kept showing up to school because she believed that would be the case. Instead, school not only failed to adequately intervene on Monique's behalf, but in fact punitive policies and practices constrained her ability to make forward academic progress. I open with Monique's story to ground this work in the real dilemmas facing everyone who endeavors to learn in, teach in, lead, or improve urban public schools, and to keep in view the human costs of unwittingly shutting the doors of opportunity on earnest but imperfect teenagers. Our need to act is urgent, before we fail yet another generation of Moniques who may well have succeeded in a more wisely built system.

THE LIVES OF ADOLESCENTS AND THE ASSUMPTIONS OF HIGH SCHOOL

I've worked in and with public high schools across the country, as a high school teacher and administrator, a college faculty member, and an educational policy researcher. I helped design, open, and run a charter high school and, with my colleagues, tried to craft innovative policies and systems that would yield a better set of results. I've also watched my own two daughters negotiate the terrain of urban public high schools in two different cities. Throughout these experiences, I have paid particular attention to failure.

By and large, I think students who fail out of urban schools are very much like my young friend Monique. They have good hearts and good intentions. They want to do well in the world. They care about school, they care about their futures, and they keep showing up. When they fail, they "try, try again" to get an education. And yet, a stunning number of these students end up turning bitter and dropping out instead of catching up and finishing high school. Why? Certainly, like Monique's, their lives are often complicated by inequalities dictated by race and class (both of which, like public schools, are social creations not of their making). And certainly, being teenagers, they make mistakes. They choose unwisely. They act irrationally and irresponsibly. As the mother of two teenagers, I'm pretty sure that's just what teenagers do. I look at Monique, and I see so many other kids I know.

The difference is not that some students care and others don't, or that some students make mistakes and others do not. When I look back on my own experience in adolescence, I know my relative educational success was so very dependent on privileges and advantages afforded to me as a middle-class White kid with an intact family and adults who bailed me out when I acted my age. And they definitely had to bail me out, as I have had to bail out my own children. What happens when a child has no such privilege or advantage, no one to advocate on her behalf, no one to give her the benefit of the doubt, and no one to step in when she makes poor decisions?

Schools seem to operate on the expectation that students' lives will not interfere with their academic work. Teachers set rules, deadlines, and grading policies to enforce the primacy of schoolwork, but those policies do not prevent circumstance from undermining students' academic efforts. Then the sharp edge of those policies comes crashing down, generally in the form of the letter F, the system's ultimate tool or weapon. Student failure is the combined product of age-old structures designed to facilitate selectivity and of seemingly benign classroom policies and practices, implemented by well-meaning educators with students' best interests in mind, that ultimately make it nearly impossible for failing kids to get back on track.

THE PREVALENCE OF HIGH SCHOOL FAILURE

In order to learn from our failure, we have to understand its breadth, depth, and recurring patterns. The extent of academic failure in high schools is apparent in four closely related links in an unfortunate chain. First, the number of students who fail individual high school courses is alarmingly high. Second, failure is evidenced by credit deficiency and, third, by grade retention. National enrollment numbers balloon in the first year of high school as students enter 9th grade with their age cohort but get stuck there due to failed courses and credit deficiencies. High school dropout is the fourth and ultimate form of failure. A brief examination of statistics from cities around the country reveals not only the prevalence of high school failure, but also the pivotal importance of students' academic performance in 9th grade.

Ninth-Grade Course Failure as the First Link in a Chain

Students entering high school are subject to a new type of accountability: To advance through school and graduate, they must earn credits by passing courses. The first level of high school failure for which there are real consequences, then, is course failure. Failing classes impedes forward progress and puts a student behind in the necessary accumulation of course credits. Course failure has two additional costs: Down the road, an F on one's permanent transcript sends a warning signal to college admissions officers or potential employers. Each F also depresses a student's GPA by averaging 0.0 grade points in the calculation, often disqualifying students from scholarships or admission to more selective (and generally better) colleges or training programs.

Unfortunately, just when passing classes and earning good grades really start to "count," students' average grades go down and course failures go up. Commonly over half the freshmen in urban school systems fail at least one course in a major subject; about a third of students fail three or more courses (Allensworth & Easton, 2007; Legters, Balfanz, Jordan, & McPartland, 2002; Neild & Weiss, 1999). Interestingly, even students with good test scores and no previous Fs have significant 9th-grade failure rates. Of Chicago students who entered high school *performing at grade level* in reading and math, almost a third failed a core course in their first semester of high school. Of high-achieving students, those whose performance had been well above average in 8th grade, a quarter failed a core 9th-grade course (Roderick & Camburn, 1999). These data paint a picture of systematic failure upon entry to high school, even among clearly capable students. And course failure has surprisingly stark ramifications. In Chicago, for example, a 9th-grader's probability of graduating drops by 15 percentage points with each failed semester course (Allensworth & Easton, 2007). Students who fail one full-year course in 9th grade see their odds of graduating decrease by 30%.

Credit Deficiency as the Result of Course Failure

Students earn credits by passing courses. When they fail courses, they become credit deficient, and credit deficiency decreases the odds that students will earn a diploma. In the state of Oregon, students who left high school without graduating cited credit deficits more than any other single factor as their primary reason for dropping out of school (Oregon State Department of Education, 2000). In Ontario, Canada, the "vast majority of dropouts left school because they were so far behind in credit accumulation that the likelihood of graduation was too remote" (King, Warren, Michalski, & Pearlt, 1988, p. 3). The importance of on-pace credit accumulation prompted Marshall (2003) to identify 9th grade as "the pivotal year" in determining high school success or failure.

On one hand, this seems intuitively obvious: Students need credits to graduate, so not earning credits reduces the likelihood of graduating. What is not so obvious is why credit deficiency is such a seemingly permanent state. In most school systems, high school students enroll in more classes than they need for graduation. For example, Chicago students take 7 or 8 credits per year for 4 years but only need 24 credits to graduate, an average of 6 per year. Seattle students typically enroll in 6 classes annually but need only 20 credits to graduate. Although graduation requirements also include specific course requirements (4 years of English, 3 years of math, and so forth), there is "wiggle room" built into students' schedules that should allow them to easily recover credits lost to a few failed courses. Furthermore, in virtually every district, students can attend night school or summer school to recover missing credits, and they can retake a failed class in a later term. Increasingly, schools are offering online courses as another route to credit recovery. A large number of students pursue these options each year. So why is credit deficiency something from which few students recover?

Michelle Fine's (1991) study in New York City sheds light on this question. Students can recover missing credits, but this takes time. As their peers advance, credit-deficient students repeat classes. Fine draws from extensive interviews to describe students' experience of this phenomenon: "First they 'feel tall,' then 'embarrassed to be sittin' next to my baby brother in class.' They eventually describe 'feelin' stupid and out of place'" (p. 238). Farrell (1990) described the "desperate" calculus of credit deficiency, observing that credit-deficient students "know how many credits they have and how many they need. Moreover, they know how many they are likely to earn each semester. The 17-year-old ninth-grader [who] cannot graduate before he reaches his twenty-first birthday" is likely to give up on earning a diploma (p. 94).

These studies paint a picture of students who see a darkening forest for the trees. As eager 14-year-olds grow older and recovering each credit takes another year of life, their focus switches from individual failures to an overall pattern of diminishing returns. They find themselves clawing their way forward but getting further behind. Eventually, students recognize the futility of staying in school.

Retention in Ninth Grade as a Critical Blow

The image of the 17-year-old freshman illuminates the next stop on the road to dropout. When 9th-graders fail multiple courses, they don't have enough credits to advance to 10th grade. Thus, the number of students "retained in grade" is the third indicator of pervasive high school failure. In Philadelphia, for example, about half of the district's first-time 9th-graders did not earn enough credits to be promoted at year's end (Neild & Weiss, 1999). Holding students back in 9th grade contributes to a phenomenon in which the size of 9th-grade enrollment (in a given high school or nationally) is disproportionate to the size of 8th- and 10th-grade enrollments. One would expect a fair degree of consistency within large populations in the number of students enrolled from one grade or year to the next, but researchers have observed a perpetual "9th-grade bubble" in the United States. West (2009) traced the annual enrollment numbers for the national student cohort that entered 1st grade in 1996 and graduated in spring 2008. Each year, from 1st through 8th grades, enrollment numbers hovered around 3.75 million students. In 9th grade, however, the number of pupils rose dramatically, to more than 4.25 million, as students from the incoming Class of 2008 were added in with students from previous cohorts who were still stuck in freshman year. After 9th grade, enrollment numbers decreased steadily each year as students dropped out of school, ending with just over 2.75 million diploma recipients out of the 3.75 million who started in that cohort (West, 2009).

In looking at U.S. enrollment data from slightly earlier cohorts, Wheelock and Miao (2005) found 13% more students in 9th grade nationally in 2001 than had been in 8th grade the previous year. Tenth-grade enrollment was 11–12% smaller than the previous year's 9th-grade figures. Across the country, this adds up to big numbers. In 2000, the 9th-grade population nationally had 440,000 more students than were in 8th grade and 520,000 more students than were in 10th grade that year. This bubble pattern was consistent over several years' time, with the number of enrolled students increasing from 8th to 9th grades each year and then decreasing significantly again as each cohort moved to 10th grade.

This "9th-grade bubble" phenomenon is seen across all races but appears particularly pronounced for African Americans and Latinos. Wheelock and Miao found that for every year between 1992 and 2001, national 9th-grade enrollment for White students was consistently 6–8% higher than White 8th-grade enrollment. But for African American students across that time span, annual differences in 8th- and 9th-grade enrollments were 23–27%. Likewise, 24–28% more Latino students were in 9th grade than in 8th grade each year, suggesting that minority students were significantly more likely than White students to be retained in 9th grade and/or to be stuck there for multiple years.

Grade retention has serious long-term ramifications. In New York, being retained once in 9th grade almost doubled the likelihood that students would never reach 10th grade and almost tripled the likelihood they would drop out (Fine, 1991). Drawing on data across 26 states, Haney (2000) concluded that 7 of every 10 freshmen without sufficient credits for promotion to 10th grade would eventually drop out of school.

In districts across the country, 9th grade in urban high schools acts as something of a backwater eddy in which failing students get caught and whirl around a bit before passing enough courses and earning sufficient credits to break free and move to the 10th grade. Evidenced by national enrollment and dropout rates, however, a large percentage of those students never recover from initial 9th-grade course failure. A misleading statistic characterizes 9th grade as the year students are most likely to drop out of school. In fact, relatively few students leave high school during their first year of enrollment. What actually happens is that a large percentage of eventual dropouts were in high school for multiple years before leaving. They just never made it out of 9th grade.

High School Dropout as the Ultimate Failure

School failure at its most catastrophic level in the United States is evidenced by an epidemic of high school dropouts. Despite free access to public schools and compulsory attendance laws, huge numbers of students fail to complete a basic K–12 education. Swanson (2010) calculated a national high school completion rate of only 68.8% for the class of 2007. Urban high schools typically lose about half their minority students prior to graduation. National graduation rates average 54% for African Americans, 56% for Latinos, and 51% for American Indians, compared with 77% for Whites and 81% for Asians (Swanson, 2010).[1] The districts with the lowest graduation rates are all located in large cities and graduate fewer than half their students on time (Greene, 2001/2002). By every indicator, rampant failure is pervasive in high school, a ubiquitous feature of secondary education in America.

PAYING ATTENTION TO NINTH-GRADE FAILURE

The first lesson of high school failure is that 9th grade is a pivotal year. Whether our interest is in improving the prospects of individual students, preparing a capable citizenry for democratic society, uplifting historically disenfranchised communities, equipping young people with knowledge and skills to contribute to our national prosperity in a competitive global economy, or simply developing tools to solve problems facing the coming generation—each of these outcomes rests heavily on students' success in the 1st year of high school, when educational trajectories seem to be set.

In response to accumulating evidence about freshman course failure, schools and districts have enacted policies and practices focused on improving students' transition to high school by providing targeted supports. Some high schools have created "9th-grade academies" offering more personal attention and academic assistance to incoming freshmen. Several large districts have implemented "early warning" systems to closely scrutinize students' academic performance from the first weeks of school. Rather than waiting until 9th-graders fail, school personnel immediately intervene if grades or attendance fall below certain thresholds. These are welcome and important actions, with indications that they may well improve students' academic performance in 9th grade and beyond. In Chicago, for example, research by my colleague Melissa Roderick shows that efforts to get more students "on track" in 9th grade—through focused attention on reducing freshman course failures and absences—has resulted in direct improvements to the graduation rates of those student cohorts 4 years later (Roderick, Kelley-Kemple, Johnson, & Beechum, in press).

But we still don't know why failure in the first year of high school is so systematically predictive of dropping out later. A central goal of my research has been to shed light on this puzzle. Only by fully understanding the processes and mechanisms connecting early failure to dropout can we craft intelligent responses in policy and practice and turn around our failing institution.

FOUR DIMENSIONS OF STUDENT ACHIEVEMENT

In studying urban high school failure, I see four interrelated dimensions of student achievement that help us understand the scope and contour of failing to learn. (These are also key to solving our failure problem, as we will see in later chapters.) The first dimension is structural. High schools were largely modeled after factories, built to churn out educated schoolchildren in uniform batches. What drives the instructional process under this model is not student learning, but rather *time*—and the imperative to "cover" whatever curriculum has been allotted to each block of time. As on an assembly line, students are presented with and then evaluated on a chunk of material before moving systematically to the next unit. Time is of the essence and teachers feel enormous pressure to keep moving through, even if the pace makes it impossible for many students to actually learn. The conveyer belt keeps rolling, providing little opportunity for "trying again" at any assignment, paper, project, quiz, or test on which a student performs poorly, fails outright, or misses due to absence. Teachers record low, failing, or missing grades (zeros) in their grade books, and the class moves to the next lesson. Failure is a quality control feature in this factory model; like tossing out dented cans, Fs indicate those who could not learn in the time allowed.

The second dimension of student achievement is academic. Without the opportunity to remediate their learning when they fall short, too many students proceed through high school accumulating failing grades on assignments or tests but not really developing essential academic skills and content knowledge. The missing pieces stay missing. Students who fail an entire course are inadequately prepared for future coursework. It's hard to do well in Spanish II if you didn't learn enough to pass Spanish I, so ongoing course failure is likely.

Exacerbating this situation are the shortcomings of teenagers themselves. The particular developmental challenges of adolescents constitute the third dimension of achievement. It's no secret that teenagers can be immature. Often they haven't yet developed strategies for coping with assignments that are not inherently interesting or for recognizing when they need help and seeking it out. Adolescents at 14 and 15 years old are still developing the capacity to plan and organize complex tasks or to use abstractions about future consequences to guide their actions. Unfortunately, rather than helping students develop these capacities, skills, and strategies, high school classrooms are often organized in ways that simply punish students for not already having them. Giving students low grades because of poor organizational skills does not actually teach them how to be better organized. Coupled with inadequate opportunities to "try again," failing students might mark a lot of time in school without actually developing the self-regulatory and organizational skills that would allow them to do better. This developmental dimension is a critical component of high school failure, particularly in 9th grade.

The fourth dimension of student achievement—and the fourth explanation for widespread failure—is motivational. Academic success in high school depends on hard work and effort over 4 years. Human beings have to be motivated to continue working hard over time, whether this motivation comes from within or from external sources. Teenagers (like all of us) need to see how the work they are asked to do is related to things they care about. They need social interaction and opportunities to talk about ideas and articulate their understanding. They do well when goals are clear, feedback on their performance is immediate, helpful structures are in place, and encouragement and support are plentiful. They need to believe they have a reasonable chance of succeeding at something that is hard to do. Unfortunately, the instructional conditions in most high school classrooms do not support student motivation. In fact, it must be said that if we were to intentionally design an environment to work directly *against* the motivational needs of most adolescents, we could not do better than the present American high school.

Young people entering 9th grade are preoccupied with questions of the self: Who am I? How do I fit in with those around me? What do I have to offer? What is my purpose? As do all human beings, teenagers strive for a sense of competence and belonging. They want to experience themselves as capable people with a meaningful place in the world. Under the right conditions, adolescents are perfectly positioned to *want to* engage in hard work—alone or with their peers—to accomplish great things.

We see evidence of this in places with resources to support strong arts, sports, or other youth development programs. Young people work hard every day in school orchestras, basketball games, math clubs, drill teams, tutoring programs, theater productions, service projects, debate teams, and dance troupes. We see evidence of adolescents' ability for diligence, concentration, and hard work in independent endeavors like advancing through the levels of a challenging video game, perfecting a jump shot, playing the cello, writing and rewriting poetry or stories, creating YouTube videos, caring for younger siblings, or calculating statistics for a favorite sports team. In areas that actually offer youth employment, we see teenagers working hard at their jobs. Regardless of race, ethnicity, nationality, home language, or socioeconomic level, kids across the country work hard every day in a wide variety of endeavors. Unfortunately, few if any of the conditions that support adolescents' hard work in other domains exist in most urban high school classrooms.

To exacerbate matters, when students fail in school, failure itself is constructed in a way that is not academically motivating. On the contrary, the more failure students experience, the less likely they are to put forth effort on future academic tasks. When students most need to double down on their efforts, we create conditions that make that most unlikely.

When we combine students' developmental shortcomings, the motivational conditions undermining their school performance, the structural features that drive traditional instruction and grading, and students' accumulating academic deficiencies within this system, it starts becoming clear why high schools are beset by widespread failure. We might accept that some students are just "beyond help" if we were talking about a small handful of failing kids. But when 30% of the nation's youth and virtually half the students of color drop out of high school, we have to understand this as a systemic problem—an institutional failure—and not just an assortment of unrelated, individual cases.

THE LONG-TERM CONSEQUENCES OF DROPPING OUT OF SCHOOL

High school graduates earn about $260,000 more over a lifetime than do dropouts, adding up to approximately $192 billion in lost income for every new cohort of 18-year-olds that doesn't complete high school (Rouse, 2005). Dropouts make less money both because they earn lower wages and because they are more likely to be unemployed. Consequently, dropouts are much more likely than high school graduates to depend on public assistance to survive (Jayakody, Danziger, & Pollack, 2000; Waldfogel, Garfinkel, & Kelly, 2005). Perhaps because they have a harder time earning a living in the legitimate economy, dropouts are also much more likely to commit crimes and be incarcerated than peers who complete high school (Pettit & Western, 2001; Raphael, 2004). These outcomes hold true even when researchers control for factors such as race, prior academic achievement, and family socioeconomic status.

People who drop out of high school are also less likely to participate in the political process. In the 2004 presidential election, only 40% of high school dropouts voted, compared with 56% of people with high school diplomas and 78% of college graduates (Junn, 2005). High school dropouts even die sooner than high school graduates, by an average of 9.2 years, in part because high school graduates have better access to health information and health care and can afford to live in safer neighborhoods than dropouts (Muennig, 2005). Importantly, these costs or payoffs also affect the health, development, and educational attainment of their children (Wolfe & Haveman, 2002). For students who drop out of school this year, we can expect to feel the negative repercussions well into the next generation.

POVERTY EXACERBATES FAILURE

Urban schools are disproportionately likely to serve poor and minority students, and poverty makes a significant difference in the likelihood that students will quit school. The U.S. Department of Education estimates that students in the lowest-income families (of six income brackets) drop out of high school at six times the rate of students in the highest-income families (U.S. Department of Education, National Center for Education Statistics, 2004). Students from low-income families also tend to be concentrated in high-poverty districts. In 2002, the 100 largest school districts in the United States, representing less than one-tenth of 1% of the 17,000 districts nationwide, educated a full 30% of the nation's poor children (MDRC, 2002).

The level of poverty typically experienced by urban students creates material, environmental, physical, and psychological conditions that greatly increase their chances of course failure (Berliner, 2009). Mental and physical health issues, lack of child care, lack of access to transportation, unstable housing, exposure to environmental toxins, victimization from community violence, and earlier entrance into parenthood make urban students more likely to miss school and fail classes. These same conditions also disadvantage parents or guardians trying to advocate on their children's behalf with school personnel. For example, low-income wage earners are much more likely to work one or more hourly jobs with less flexibility for time off to make visits to a child's school. To the extent that low-income youth and families have fewer resources to weather challenges, disruptive life events take a disproportionate toll on the schooling trajectories of poor and minority students.

Urban public schools are sites of contradiction concerning race and class. On one hand, public education reflects our commitment to and has long embodied our best hopes for racial equality and social progress. On the other hand, urban schools seem to compound the deleterious effects of race and class, almost guaranteeing the continued reproduction of a permanent underclass. The large percentage of low-income students of color dropping out of high school without a diploma starkly calls into question our basic philosophical beliefs and commitments about the role of public education in the quest for racial and social equality.

If our goal in public high schools is to help everyone learn and ultimately to have no one fail (in the sense of failing to graduate or failing to learn enough to make a living), it seems we could structure schools to respond to initial learning failure or early course failure with additional support and resources. We could view failure as something natural and expected when students are learning new skills or pushing the limits of their current understanding. We could construct failure as an opportunity to recognize and learn from errors in thinking or acting. We could design classroom instruction to respond effectively to "failure to understand," "failure to use a strategy," "failure to develop a skill," or even "failure to do the work" before it became full-blown course failure. When students did occasionally fail a course (as some inevitably would), we could have clear, structured pathways to lead them forward to success by remediating their learning and providing effective and realistic opportunities to recover lost credits toward graduation.

But ensuring that everyone learns does not seem to be the goal of high school. Judging by existing structures and our punitive response to students who fail, academic failure seems to be the way we figure out who doesn't deserve to succeed in life. We rationalize adolescents' failure by reassuring ourselves that they brought it upon themselves: They did not try hard enough, they did not care, they couldn't get it together, or they just weren't very smart. The inevitable downward spiral of failure and decreased motivation virtually assures that students entering high school with the fewest social, economic, and academic advantages will leave with the lowest qualifications, solidifying their place at the bottom of the socioeconomic order. This is our institutional failure.

TWO

How We Got Here

Tracing the Origins of High School Failure

Learning from our failure requires that we reflect on how we got here. A central argument in this book is that high schools fail so many students in large part because that is what they were designed to do. Understanding why high schools have such high rates of failure and how those failure rates have been achieved is crucial to understanding what we need to do differently if we want to produce better outcomes for students. Looking back in history allows us to identify the origins of much of our current practice and prompts us to question many of our current assumptions.

The prototype of our modern high school came from the late 19th century when fewer than 10% of American adolescents attended secondary school and fewer yet attained a diploma. The U.S. educational system was (and still is) shaped like a pyramid, with elementary schools forming the broad base and colleges and universities at the narrow peak. The contours of that pyramid are made clear by historical enrollment data. A speaker at a National Council of Education meeting in 1897 noted that "while 50 percent of the school[-aged] population is enrolled in the public elementary schools, but 6 percent is enrolled in the high schools, while only one-half of 1 percent . . . graduates from the high schools" ("Hot day for educators," 1897).[1] That the size of the population shrank in each subsequent level of school did not particularly worry proponents of this hierarchical system. Indeed, the upper elementary and secondary schools were designed in part to winnow out the "laggards"[2] and the "dull-minded" and let the cream rise to the top.

STANDARDIZED INSTRUCTION PRODUCED WIDESPREAD FAILURE

A central challenge to high schools for over 150 years has been how to meet the needs of a diverse group of students. From their early history, high schools learned a crucial lesson in efficiency from increasingly mechanistic urban elementary classrooms: "To manage successfully a hundred children, or even half that number, the teacher must reduce them as nearly as possible to a unit" (Tyack, 1974, p. 54). Sorting students by ability and creating classrooms that were as homogeneous as possible were essential to systematizing the growing city schools. Testing and failing students were the primary mechanisms used to achieve these ends (Kaestle, 1983; Mc-Clusky, 1920). Failure flagged lower-achieving students and prevented their advancement to the next grade level. Educators hoped this would create less heterogeneity in the class the following year, making it easier to teach.

As a consequence of the actual variability of students in a system striving for uniformity, failure in 19th- and early 20th-century schools was widespread. If teachers delivered instruction in one standardized method to a wide range of students, holding constant the instructional time and method of evaluation, some percentage of student failure was virtually assured (Bloom, 1968; Carroll, 1963). As Deschenes, Tyack, and Cuban (2001) noted, "Failing and passing were defining features of bureaucratized urban education of the latter part of the nineteenth century. To a large degree failure became an artifact of the rigidity of a system that sought to process large batches of children in uniform ways" (p. 528). In a context where academic success was defined as keeping pace with your batch of peers, some students were guaranteed to fail.

In 1909, Leonard Ayres conducted the largest-ever study of school failure, examining enrollment and promotion data for 1,982,477 children in elementary and high schools in 58 cities. Though he observed significant variability across schools and cities, he found widespread failure at every grade level, estimating that, on average, 20% of students failed to be promoted each year. In tracking promotions and retentions for students in each grade, Ayres had this to report:

> In the typical first grade, for every four beginners there are three other children who are repeating the work of the grade. The second, third, fourth, and fifth grades all contain considerable proportions of repeaters. The sixth is the first grade showing any dropping out of pupils. By this grade 10 per cent have left. The seventh grade shows such a decided falling off that only 71 per cent are left. By the time the eighth grade is reached practically one-half of the pupils have dropped out. . . . The general tendency of city school systems is to keep all of the children to the fifth grade, to drop half of them by the time the eighth grade is reached and to carry one in ten to the fourth year of high school. (pp. 58–59)

Examining data from a subset of 16 cities, Ayres calculated that, of 1,000 students enrolled in school at age 14, on average 740 of them had failed at least once during their school careers. Collectively, these 740 students amassed 1,217 total failures across their years at school. "Judged by the standard of frequency," he noted, failure was "rather the rule than the exception" in every district (p. 12).

Ayres noted that grade levels were not calibrated to the average pupil. To the contrary, "the average child in the average city school system progresses through the grades at the rate of eight grades in ten years" (p. 88). He found "no 'lock-step' in the progress of pupils through the typical American city school system. What we do find is a system by which the brighter pupils move forward at the rate of a grade a year, the exceptional pupil sometimes gains a year and the average and dull pupils fail repeatedly" (p. 193). By the time most American children leave public school, Ayres wrote, "they are thoroughly trained in failure" (p. 220).

Studies focusing exclusively on high schools around the turn of the 20th century found similarly widespread levels of failure. A survey across California public high schools reported that 29% of students left high school in 1903 because they were failing classes. In some schools, over half the enrolled student body failed out of school that year (Barker, 1903/1965). Rounds and Kingsbury's 1913 study of more than 30,000 students in 46 high schools across the country found that 10.4% of students failed English that year and another 8.2% dropped out before the English final exam. In mathematics, 16.3% failed and another 8.4% dropped out before the exam.

High rates of failure meant that few students survived through 4 years of secondary education. For example, Chicago high schools in 1896 enrolled 3,278 students in 9th grade but only 870 students in 12th grade, a typical rate of attrition ("No drones among them," 1896). In its 1918 report, *Cardinal Principles of Secondary Education*, the Commission on the Reorganization of Secondary Education spelled out a central concern: "Of those who enter the four-year high school about one-third leave before the beginning of the second year, about one-half are gone before the beginning of the third year, and fewer than one-third are graduated. . . . These facts can no longer be safely ignored" (Department of the Interior, p. 8.).

MERITOCRACY RATIONALIZED WIDESPREAD FAILURE

The high rate of failure in early 20th-century high schools is particularly striking when one considers that even getting into high school was a selective process. Public high schools at the turn of the century did not actually admit just anyone. Hopeful applicants who graduated from 8th grade (already a fraction of the population) had to submit recommendation letters from elementary school principals and pass rigorous examinations to gain entry to the public high school. A large number of students who took high school entrance tests were found lacking and barred from enrolling. Newspaper reports from the time were replete with stories of harrowing entrance examinations and accounts of suicides by young people who failed them (see, for example, the *Chicago Tribune* story from 1895, "Another Suicide by Carbolic Acid"). Rigorous entrance requirements were almost universally applauded. As education historians Deschenes, Tyack, and Cuban (2001) explained, "Far from defining failures in [high school entrance] examinations as a problem, many educators saw them instead as a sign that academic standards were being maintained" (p. 528). Public high schools were designed to be very selective institutions.

How did school systems justify these differences in opportunity, providing free, taxpayer-supported secondary education to only some children in town while excluding others? The idea of *merit*, a concept "deeply etched in the American consciousness" (Bowles & Gintis, 1976, p. 103), was pivotal in securing public support for public high schools for *some*. The underlying assumption was that all children (or, as practiced in most cities, all White children) had a chance at enrollment. Students' acceptance into high school and their progress once there depended on how smart they were and how hard they worked. Virtually every structure, policy, and practice within the high school—in 1903 and still very true today—served to reify the notion that individuals were advanced and rewarded on the basis of merit. As Michael Young satirically described it, "I + E = M," intelligence plus effort equaled merit, and all social privilege and access flowed accordingly (1958/1994, p. 84).

Most people around the turn of the 20th century accepted as fact that intelligence was largely inherited and fixed at birth—whatever you came into this world with was the total of what you would ever have. Intelligence was distributed across the population in a bell-shaped curve, meaning that a few people had a whole lot, a few people had hardly any, and most people were somewhere in the middle. Accordingly, only a small percentage of the population was smart enough to finish high school. School got harder with every grade level, so each year some percentage of students would reach the limits of their natural ability and be unable to advance any further.

The notion of "grading on a curve" arose from these beliefs about fixed intelligence. A scientific treatise on grading in 1908 noted that about a quarter of the students in any class were likely to be mentally "inferior." Accordingly, "if most or all of these students fail under a particular teacher, there may be but little objection" (Meyer, 1908, p. 248). Those who failed or dropped out had simply gone as far as their intellects would take them. Lack of intelligence was also the reason given for the large number of failures in the 1903 California high school study. Wrote that study's author, "Undoubtedly many failures were due to want of ability; for the incompetent and unfortunate will always be with us" (Barker, 1903/1965, p. 80).

Intelligence was not the only component of merit, however. Character also counted. School success was determined by a combination of natural intellectual ability and effort. Hard-working students succeeded where lazy ones failed. Effort was a sign of character, but turn-of-the-century thinkers had differing theories on the determinants of character. Some believed a young person's character could be developed by religious training, hard work, or strict discipline. Others thought character was something inherent—a fixed trait like intelligence. Many prevailing beliefs linked character with race, ethnicity, or socioeconomic class. From that perspective, well-bred children of the middle and upper classes were believed to have the moral fiber to grow into upstanding adults, while children of immigrants and the working poor were seen as shiftless and problematic. For those who held this view, it was not surprising that children from more privileged families tended to put forth more effort to learn and advanced much further in school than foreigners or poor kids, who seemed to fail in great numbers. The relative academic success of more well-to-do children was taken as evidence that racist or class-based beliefs about intelligence and character were true.

As David Labaree described in *The Making of an American High School*, "meritocratic theory argues that individual differences in ability, motivation, and character define varying degrees of individual worth or merit. Accordingly, those with the most merit should receive the largest share of social rewards, and it becomes society's responsibility to guarantee that people get what they deserve" (1988, p. 23). Meritocratic principles were "meant to convince us that although we may not live in the best of all *conceivable* worlds, we live in the best of all *possible* worlds" (Lewontin, 1992, p. 21). Given our naturally varying abilities and characters, each person's possibilities are limited only by his or her own shortcomings.

At the extreme, early proponents of the selection and stratification function of education dismissed the notion of equality outright. From a social-efficiency perspective, schools could do nothing to promote equity. Rather, the goal was to expediently slot each person in his or her rightful place in the workforce. "Instead of being born free and equal," wrote Ellwood Cubberley (1919), dean of Stanford University's school of education, "we are born free and unequal, and unequal we shall ever remain. The school, we now see, cannot make intelligence; it can only train and develop and make useful the intelligence that the child brings with him to a school [from his] racial and family inheritance." If the student didn't have enough intelligence to succeed in an academic setting, it was the school's duty to determine this as early as possible and remove him from the rolls. A similar sentiment appeared in a 1920s textbook for teachers: "Nothing that education can do will enable a non-selected group of individuals to approach equality either in ability or in achievement. Indeed, it may be confidently asserted that the net result of education is to magnify differences rather than eliminate them" (Strayer & Engelhardt, 1920, quoted in Reese, 2005, pp. 155–156).

Thus, ubiquitous failure was simply a sign things were working correctly: Schools were sorting the wheat from the chaff. As a 1913 article in *The School Review* noted, "the teacher in whose classes a comparatively low percentage of pupils passed was considered good on the basis of this fact alone. He was given the name of being a man of high standards and rigorous requirements" (Rounds & Kingsbury, p. 597). Only a subset of students who entered high school actually possessed the intelligence or put forth the effort to succeed. Those with the necessary brains and moral character were rewarded with further opportunity. But there was no point in wasting education on intellectually or morally inferior students. For anxious taxpayers, a self-protective middle class, and a fledgling teaching profession, student failure was evidence of quality control.

The historical literature makes clear that, rather than being concerned about widespread failure, many educators and taxpayers were much more worried about "unfit" high school students who were not capable of profiting from secondary education. In the late 1890s and the first decades of the 20th century, taxpayers were being asked to foot the bill for an exploding number of public high schools—a growing new expense for local governments. Newspapers and educational journals at the time were filled with articles about "waste" of public funds on students who could not properly benefit from formal instruction.

To that end, the Board of Education in Berkeley, California, set a policy in 1907 that "high school students, hereafter, who fail to pass examinations in any two studies will be dropped" from enrollment ("Berkeley teachers," 1907, p. 7). An 1896 meeting of the Chicago Board of Education sought stricter high school admission requirements "so the schools may be thinned out . . . and elevated in character" ("Too many poor pupils," 1896). The author of a 1917 study in Kansas City concluded that students who failed high school algebra were of "subnormal" intelligence and that remedial classes were "a waste of public-school funds [and] should be eliminated" (Wood, 1920). Rounds and Kingsbury (1913) came to the same conclusion in their national study of high schools. For the sake of students, parents, and taxpayers, "there can be no question that the ends of justice and wisdom will best be served by the failure of some of these pupils" (p. 596). There was little point in trying to educate students who proved their academic inadequacy.

The public high school was a meritocratic testing ground, where all had a shot at entrance but only the most capable or most dedicated students would gain admittance, advance to the highest levels, and reap the greatest rewards (Eliot, 1909; Tyack, 1974). Those who failed simply did not have the stuff for the academic arena; they were better off leaving school to seek their livelihood in the world of work. This process of "natural selection" was essential because nobody knew how to accurately predict who would do well in school. Taxpayers could only be induced to pay for public high schools if they believed their own children might have the opportunity to attend. They agreed to a system of educating all who showed promise and advancing students on the basis of their academic success.

Student failure thus assisted the high school in fulfilling one of its long-standing purposes in American culture: identifying and certifying qualified students for higher education and the labor market (Meyer & Rowan, 1983). By granting diplomas to only a small subset of students, the monetary value of the credential was ensured for those rare few who obtained it. If standards were lowered and high school diplomas became more common, they would lose their currency. High failure rates protected the payoff to completing high school.

Besides protecting the value of a diploma, failure in secondary schools also served the purposes of the colleges. Colleges and universities saw it as their mission to select the best and brightest of the next generation and prepare them for civic and intellectual leadership roles. Gatekeeping mechanisms in high schools served the explicit function of stratifying student achievement, allowing colleges to select the best from a pool of worthy, qualified applicants. Identifying students most likely to succeed in higher education evolved as a central purpose of secondary education. Much of the apparatus that supported that purpose became a cornerstone to the modern high school.

TIME, GRADES, AND CREDITS DEFINED
ACADEMIC SUCCESS AND FAILURE

It is all well and good to have beliefs and social values that guide a system, but what were the mechanisms whereby such beliefs and values were set in motion? How did the concepts of meritocracy, natural intelligence, effort, and character get translated into systems that produced success and failure? Today, we take for granted all the traditional structures that select and stratify student achievement: semesters, grades, credits, report cards, transcripts. These are the mechanisms by which all students were (and are) sorted and selected for advanced opportunity. Features of this traditional system include: grouping students by age as they enter the public school system; dividing school years into marking periods of a fixed length (e.g., quarters or semesters); repeating teach-and-test sequences throughout the year; using points or letter grades to quantify and evaluate each piece of student work; averaging points or letters to determine final course grades;

awarding course credit for a passing grade and denying credit for a failing one; advancing students on the basis of credit accumulation; averaging final course grades into grade point averages (GPAs); using grade point averages to determine class rankings; and using grades, credits, GPA, class rank, and, in some cases, scores on specialized or standardized tests to determine future educational opportunity. These are the structures, policies, and practices that have always ensured that only the best and the brightest would emerge victorious. In our reflection on how we got to our current state of failure in urban high schools, let us briefly examine some of the elements of this system and ponder their ongoing role in selection and stratification.[3]

Letter Grades, Grade Point Averages, and Class Rank

The genius of the traditional grading system is its efficiency: Across a complex set of interactions involving hundreds of hours of instruction and student activity and a broad swath of course content, a student's learning within a semester course is reduced to a single letter grade. Because most teachers average together a number of grades from assignments, quizzes, homework, and longer-term projects to arrive at a final course grade, much information is lost about the individual student's performance in class. What grades do well is distinguish top performers: The only way to earn an A is to consistently generate top-level work such that your marks *average out* to 90% or above. Even if *most* of your marks are in that top range, a couple of low scores can easily knock your final grade down to a B, C, or D. Note, too, the much wider range of opportunity to earn an F. Where all other grades have a bandwidth of about 10 percentage points (90 or above is an A, 80–89 is a B, 70–79 is a C, and so on), students who end up with anything between 0 and 59 get an F.

The downside of distilling all of one's coursework into a single letter grade is that the grade becomes a virtually meaningless abstraction. Letter grades provide no information about a learner's individual strengths or weaknesses or about the material she has mastered or failed to master (Spady, 1992; Wrinkle, 1935). Knowing how one's grades are related to one's work is fundamental to improved student performance (Assessment Reform Group, 2002; Black & Wiliam, 2004). If, as Brookhard (2004) noted, "the primary purpose for grading . . . should be to communicate with students and parents about their achievement of learning goals" and to "convey interpretable, appropriate information" about that achievement (p. 2), then letter grades just might fall short. We rely on these opaque, summative evaluations that emphasize students' relative performance rather than providing useful feedback to support their learning.

GPA is similarly uninformative. As the name implies, a student's *grade point average* is merely an averaging of course grades, generally converted to a 4-point scale, with an A worth 4 points and an F worth zero. Grade point averages were designed for a specific purpose, and that they do well: They clearly identify students whose performance is consistently stellar (or consistently poor). Its discriminatory power makes the GPA a popular tool for determining students' eligibility for colleges and scholarships. Thus, for the student with consistently stellar performance, a GPA has bankable value. In most other cases, however, GPA both obfuscates a nuanced assessment of a student's academic performance (including changes in performance over time) and directly limits his or her future opportunities.

Take the hypothetical case of "Maribel" who entered 9th grade with weak academic skills, murky future goals, and a relative lack of maturity. Let's say Maribel failed or barely passed some 9th-grade classes. Let us embellish to imagine a good scenario where reform efforts and increased academic standards dramatically improved Maribel's high school, and she responded positively to higher expectations, improved instruction, and more effective curriculum. Maribel worked hard and took advantage of educational opportunities to build the skills and knowledge she lacked when she entered high school. Her grades improved from Ds and Fs in 9th grade to Cs and Bs in 10th and 11th grades, and then to all As by her senior year. Unfortunately, when Maribel's initial underperformance was averaged together with her later academic success, her cumulative high school GPA would be about a C, likely too mediocre to qualify Maribel for merit-based scholarships or admission to good colleges.

For students like Maribel who show academic progress over time, GPA is inherently unforgiving. The assumption of the past 2 decades of education reform—with its emphasis on test-based accountability and now test-based teacher evaluation—is that increased pressure on schools and teachers will force instructional improvements that will bring underperforming students "up to standards." But even if this *works*, it happens over time. Students entering high school in the bottom quartile of academic achievement do not immediately reach higher standards. Instead, they frequently fall short of the mark, at least in their early high school coursework. And the higher we set the mark, the more failures students will accumulate before they reach it, even if they are steadily improving. An averaging of grades ensures that students' *substandard* performance will be permanently recorded on their transcripts and perpetually calculated against them in their high school GPA. If students have several low but passing grades, they reach a point pretty early on where even perfect performance thereafter would not earn them the kind of GPA they would need to qualify for competitive postsecondary opportunities.

Grade point average as a structural mechanism has a strong constituency. The use of high school GPA to predict college and work success is well documented (Bowen, Chingos, & McPherson, 2009; Geiser & Santelices,

2007; Roderick, Nagaoka, & Allensworth, 2006). Because of its predictive value, it serves well its primary audience: the college admissions officers. GPA lies at the heart of our meritocratic system of educational opportunity and functions exactly as intended within that system. But there is a fundamental contradiction between meritocracy (excellence for some) and equity and excellence for all.

While acknowledging the predictive value of GPA, we must also question the implications of this structural mechanism that discriminates between those who take 4 years to bring themselves up from underachievement and those who come into high school already earning top grades. Studies have long shown that academic performance is highly correlated with socioeconomic status and parental education levels (Farkas, 2003; Lee & Burkam, 2002). By rewarding those who enter high school with strong performance, GPA reinforces privilege. It also masks upward academic mobility by averaging in a student's academic starting point with what he or she ultimately achieves. Grade point average is an integral piece of the traditional high school system implemented for the sake of colleges and the college-bound, but it has little inherent value—and causes much potential harm—to the rest of the high school population, even to those students who successfully make the transition over time from underperformance to solid achievement.

Class rank is yet another perverse mechanism of selection and stratification in the traditional structure of achievement. Within a graduating cohort, every student's GPA is lined up from greatest to smallest (often to five or six decimal places out) and each student is assigned a place in line. This absurd ritual bestows legitimacy on the numerically dubious distinction between a GPA of 3.9478 and 3.9487. More important, what is the purpose of calculating a class rank for every member of a graduating class anyway? Being in the top 10% of one's class has bankable value for those top 10%. Perhaps students in the top half derive some comfort knowing they are better off than those below. But for the 50% of each graduating class in the bottom half, class rank may be just another humiliating indicator of one's lack of "merit," regardless of how far students have come in their learning or how much they actually know.

Time-Based Instruction and Carnegie Units

Students who wish to graduate from high school in 4 years must keep pace by accumulating a set portion of credits each year, awarded on the basis of "seat time." Since 1906, the Carnegie unit has been the measure of "time served" in high school, standardized at the rate of one course credit per 120 hours of instruction. Most state boards of education, state legislatures, or individual school districts specify minimum graduation requirements in terms of the Carnegie unit or its equivalent (e.g., 4 credits of English, 3 credits of math). Students who do not pass classes become "credit-deficient" relative to their peers and the normative path of progress, seriously reducing their probability of graduating from high school.

The role of the Carnegie unit in structuring academic achievement is hard to overestimate. We divide the 4 years of high school into courses and terms, and (sometimes vaguely) specify what students need to learn in each allotted term. We devote only so much time to each bit of content. If a student is absent or doesn't master the material in the allotted time, there is little to be done. The lesson has been taught, and the class moves on. Further, the overall terms are long. If a student falls too far behind, he generally has to wait a few months to fail the class before he can start it again.

Students who dutifully occupy their seats for the duration of a term and earn at least a D are awarded credit for the course. Students with an F as a final grade earn no credit, generally meaning they have wasted about 5 months for each failed semester course. To retrieve a credit lost to failure, students must retake the entire semester class. Students who fail multiple classes must make up multiple credits by retaking multiple courses. This is on top of the average load of six or seven classes that most students already take each term.

Let's think this through for a moment. Students who are the least academically successful, least adept at managing multiple academic demands, and/or least able to succeed in school in the face of pressing outside challenges—students who demonstrated this by failing classes—will now have to take more classes per term in order to keep up. They will have even more demands, more things to juggle, and more challenges. Essentially, we expect them to somehow *do better* under worse conditions, though we provide no additional supports and do nothing to increase their capacity to manage this workload. And why do we do it this way? Because we have accepted seat time and the Carnegie unit as central organizing principles of high school instruction. High schools are locked into this structure of time-bound instructional terms, and educators struggle within it to meet the needs of students for whom learning is not coming along at the pace of instruction. Because courses are considered inviolate units, when students fall behind or fall short, they have to start the course over from the beginning.

Beyond the obvious problem—that we are systematically setting up failing kids for further failure—there is another underlying issue. In most high schools in the country, students earn credits for classes they "pass" where the minimum passing grade is a D. The grade of D is a strange designation in between failing and actually knowing something. Far too many students in urban public schools proceed through high school passing classes with Ds but never developing the requisite knowledge and skills to succeed in subsequent classes—let alone to gain admittance to college or secure gainful employment.

Some credit-deficient students might eventually manage to graduate, but they tend to do so without having learned much. Why? Because when students fall off-pace in accumulating credits, the *acquisition of credits* becomes the de facto goal of school. Any idea of mastering course material or building subject-area expertise flies out the window, as students readjust their aim to earn the minimum passing grade in as many courses as possible as quickly as they can. We reinforce this mentality by making D a passing grade in the first place. From my vantage point, the availability of a D grade in urban high schools is basically our admission that we are not committed to teaching large numbers of students to an adequate level of understanding. In short, students who fall behind in credit accumulation are not only at great risk of dropping out of school; even if they manage to recover lost credits and graduate, they will probably leave with very little mastery of the knowledge and skills they went to high school to learn.

For example, among students who graduated between 2003 and 2005 from Chicago Public Schools (CPS), 25% finished high school with an average GPA of 1.51, a D average. Across *all* CPS graduates the average GPA was 2.36, a low C (Roderick, Coca, Moeller, & Kelley-Kemple, 2013). And these are high school *graduates*. The GPAs of those who drop out of school are appreciably lower. By structuring achievement and academic advancement around measures of seat time and credit accumulation, high schools guarantee not only that a large percentage of students will drop out, but also that a large percentage of students will graduate with few requisite skills and knowledge. The current system does not support the development of academic excellence in the vast majority of urban students.

For over 100 years, educators have argued for some alternative to this standardized approach to counting time as a way of measuring schooling. In 1902 Francis Parker called the awarding of credits for seat time a "pernicious scheme of bribery" (p. 760). University of Chicago professor Charles Judd complained in 1914 that the Carnegie unit was "a cover for defects," lamenting that "counting credits is more absorbing to the average student than mastering intellectual problems" (p. 664). Commenting on a 1933 national survey of high schools, Leonard Koos noted the "chief obstruction to reform" in secondary education was "the too great respect for the Carnegie unit," proclaiming it was "high time that [it] be discarded" (p. 507). In 1934, Forrest Long called for "at once discard[ing] the Carnegie unit" so schools could be "freed from the restrictive influence of marks, and promotion, and units" and could "begin to think in terms of human needs" (pp. 579–581). (For additional criticisms, see Aikin, 1942; Lawrence, 1965; Tompkins & Gaumnitz, 1954; and White & Duker, 1973.)

Despite longstanding recognition of the constraints it places on secondary education, the Carnegie unit still structures the daily work of teachers and students all over the country and contributes substantially to our epidemic of high school failure.

Transcripts

If Carnegie units structure high school performance, transcripts permanently record that performance. An academic transcript is the official, permanent record of a student's achievement across high school. Once a course grade is entered on a transcript, the student's level of achievement in that subject matter is fixed in time. The permanency of transcripts has two disadvantages. First, once a very low but passing grade is recorded, the student has no opportunity or incentive to revisit the material. The credit has been earned, and learning more "old" material wouldn't change the recorded grade anyway. Furthermore, short of retaking the entire course (which you can't do if you've already passed it), there are no structured opportunities to learn what was left unlearned at semester's end.

The second problem with permanent transcripts is that students can never really outrun previous failure. Even if the student responds to a failed course by retaking the exact same class and earning a good grade, in many school districts her original failing grade would still remain a permanent feature on her academic record and would be forever calculated into her cumulative GPA. Often, students make up failed credits by taking slightly different courses. In this case, the failed course most definitely remains on the transcript.

Some argue that, because grades are permanently recorded on a transcript and forever factored into GPA calculations, students develop a fear of failure that motivates them to work harder and earn higher grades (Ebel, 1980). That may be true for some students. However, for students who enter high school with an established history of underperformance or who get blindsided by the change in expectations from grade school to high school, the permanency of low or failing grades has only deleterious effects, both psychologically and materially (Covington & Müeller, 2001; Crooks, 1988; Weiner, 1979).

Time-based instructional periods, grades, credits, transcripts, GPA, and class rank are structural features of high schools that act as sorting mechanisms to distinguish top performers from everybody else. Historically, they evolved to perpetuate a meritocratic system, reinforcing ideas of individual educational achievement as they promoted stratification. These basic high school structures still serve a clear selection function today, differentiating categories of performance and then rewarding students in the top categories. These are defining features of our American high school.

THE LIMITS OF MERITOCRACY

Deeply engrained notions of meritocracy and individualism still justify our system of schooling. In effect, we believe that some people naturally "are"— or through personal effort "make themselves"—better than others. Those who garner their personal resources to the greatest effect deserve a larger portion of the spoils of American society, expressed in opportunity, status, wealth, and power. Those who fail, well, we can't keep throwing money down the drain to educate them if they can't or won't put in the effort to learn. Americans have perceived this as fair because it is based on a "most basic assumption" about academic achievement: that "what we learn is a function of both our talents—our aptitude for particular kinds of learning—and how hard we try—our effort" (Resnick, 1995, p. 55). While we don't control how much natural ability we have, neither is that subject to the control of others. And only we control our efforts. Meritocracy is thus "a 'natural' sorting process of who gets to be wealthy and powerful . . . and creates a commonsense notion about difference, inferring that those without power cannot and will never acquire power because of their own innate deficiencies" (Oakes, Wells, Jones, & Datnow, 1977, p. 485).

The concept of meritocracy has also had its critics all along—from its very origins. In a satirical novel,[4] British sociologist Michael Young (1958/1994) minted the word *meritocracy* and contrasted it with another potential approach to education and social ordering. This alternative approach would not offer "equal opportunity to rise up in the social scale, but equal opportunity for all people, irrespective of their 'intelligence,' to develop the virtues and talents with which they are endowed" (p. 160). Imagine an education system organized to ensure that each young person would "develop his own special capacities for leading a rich life" (p. 159) rather than one that required children to compete with one another for access to higher education and greater economic opportunity. By embracing meritocracy and rationalizing inequality, we "abandon more egalitarian distributional principles" (Lister, 2006, p. 233) that might be used to create a more effective educational system and a more egalitarian society.

Another criticism is this: Meritocracy rests on the false assumption that everyone is getting a fair shot, but we all know that the playing field is rarely level. Those with advantage almost always keep their advantage in a meritocratic system. In tracing the development of Philadelphia's Central High School through the 19th century, Labaree (1988) described the way meritocracy both functioned as intended (determining advancement based on merit, with the appearance of fairness) and simultaneously privileged students from middle-class families. Because the school was widely recognized to be meritocratic, Labaree wrote, its credentials were seen to mean something. But "Central's meritocracy was based entirely on formal procedures of academic selection, which applied only to those students whose class background provided them with the economic and cultural capacity to enter the contest in the first place" (p. 38). The American high school in the latter half of the 19th century allowed middle-class parents to pass along their privileged social status to their children without those less fortunate calling foul. The high school thus "provided them with a double benefit, privileged access and legitimate credentials" (p. 38).

Critics point to the tight correlation between wealth and "merit," coupled with the persistence of concentrated poverty across generations of families, concluding that the notion of "educational meritocracy is largely symbolic," with little bearing on the way wealth, power, or opportunity are actually distributed across the population (Bowles & Gintis, 1976, p. 103). And yet we still believe in meritocracy. In studying American high schools in the latter 20th century, Oakes et al. (1977) noted the sharp "contradiction between an espoused ideology of equality and meritocracy and the reality of extreme inequality" (p. 485). Resolving this contradiction "necessitated reconceptualizing the notion of equality, toward equality of opportunity rather than result" (p. 485). If it is believed that everyone has an equal shot at the prize, no one can be blamed if the prize is not equally distributed.

Even if we know meritocracy results in inequality, we still embrace it, with a vengeance. Social psychologists recently examined the notion that Americans "want to believe that hard work leads to success not simply because it is sometimes true, and not simply because it makes them feel better about themselves, but also because it helps to rationalize existing inequalities in society and preserve a view of the social system as fair and just" (Ledgerwood, Mandisodza, Jost, & Pohl, 2011, p. 322). Through a series of experiments, the team found, for example, that participants made biased judgments about scientific studies, judging "the same research evidence as higher in quality when it supported (vs. opposed) the notion that hard work leads to success," and that they were even more strongly biased after they read a passage that was critical (rather than supportive) of the idea of meritocracy. This was true even among "individuals who explicitly disavowed a personal belief in meritocracy" (p. 330). In other experiments, participants worked harder to solve a puzzle when told the study was "about the relationship between effort and doing well in American society," compared to participants who thought the study was about the relationship between effort and doing well on a puzzle. Interestingly, the participants who worked the hardest were the group whose instructions included a criticism of meritocracy. They were told, "Just like in our society," success on the puzzle was "mainly a result of luck. In other words, no matter how hard people try, they don't tend to do any better" (pp. 331–332). That group put in the most effort to solve the puzzle. The researchers concluded that Americans are motivated to justify meritocracy and will employ "defensive cognitive and behavioral processes to protect and bolster the notion that hard work leads to success in society, even in the face of contradictory evidence" (p. 337).

Our belief in meritocracy persists not only despite inequitable outcomes, but also despite clearly inequitable inputs. Students are held individually accountable for their academic achievement, regardless of resources or conditions within classrooms, schools, families, or neighborhoods that may impact their performance. Whether one attends an affluent suburban school with well-equipped classrooms and well-educated teachers or an underfunded urban school with dilapidated portable outbuildings and teachers with emergency credentials, academic achievement is constructed as a distinctly individual accomplishment. Meritocracy remains the basis upon which we decide who deserves access to better (and more lucrative) educational opportunities, such as enrollment in publicly funded magnet schools, a seat in Advanced Placement classes in high schools, college merit scholarships, and admission to the country's most elite universities.

In the Chicago Public Schools, as in other large urban districts, we decide who deserves admission to coveted public selective enrollment high schools—some of the top schools in the state—through a meritocratic system. For the 2012–2013 academic year, more than 14,000 Chicago 8th-graders competed for 3,200 freshman slots in these schools (Ahmed-Ullah, 2012). Though over 85% of CPS students are African American or Latino, the superior grades and test scores of White and Asian students mean that Whites take 25% of seats in CPS selective enrollment high schools and Asians take another 10%,[5] more than twice their proportion in the system. From a meritocratic standpoint, this is totally fair: Smart and hard-working students *deserve* opportunities that are rightfully withheld from those who don't put in the effort or don't have the "stuff."

Psychologist Norman Feather (1999) explored the idea of "deservingness" in different contexts through a variety of experiments. He found that Americans think people generally "got what they deserved" if good outcomes followed good behavior or bad outcomes followed bad behavior. In school, we see students as deserving of a high grade (good outcome) if they worked hard in class (good behavior), and we think they don't deserve a high grade (good outcome) if they cheated to get it (bad behavior). Conversely, low grades (bad outcome) are seen to be deserved if they follow from bad behavior like skipping class, but we think low grades (bad outcome) are not deserved if students worked hard in studying for an exam (good behavior). Reflecting our general notions of fairness, people are generally "seen not to deserve outcomes for which they are not responsible" (Feather, p. 5), such as students who fail an exam due to illness, but to deserve outcomes brought about by their own behavior.

However, as "we might expect," Feather wrote, our conceptions of deservingness and merit also depend on how we view a person's "character." Our judgments regarding deservingness are swayed by whether or not we like a person or approve of his or her behavior, and likewise whether or not we are members of the same social group. Feather found that we tend to like our own—to believe that "people like us" deserve the good things they get and don't deserve bad things—and to look more harshly and suspiciously on "other" social groups. When "those people" get less opportunity or reward, we are ready to believe they somehow must deserve less.

Age-old ideas of intelligence and character combined with concepts of meritocracy and deservingness largely shape our sense of what is natural and fair within the educational realm. We accept that educational opportunities are in limited supply, so we restrict access to them on the basis of merit. To determine access to education on the basis of skin color, gender, or social class has fallen out of favor, and we worry that opening the floodgates to everybody would be wasteful. So we make public K–12 schooling universally available, and those who work the hardest and are the most intellectually and academically qualified will prove their merit and rise to the top, where they become eligible for more and better opportunities. We accept this as the most fair and efficient mechanism for distributing social advantage, even though it largely serves to maintain the status quo, in part because we believe, at the end of the day, that things get sorted out fairly and accurately. For those at the top of the heap, meritocracy has the added benefit of bestowing legitimacy on the disproportionate share of wealth and power they enjoy. Despite the fact that academic achievement is highly correlated with socioeconomic status and skin color, deep down we still seem to believe that folks get what they deserve.

THREE

What We Now Know About Learning

In attempting in these pages to cull lessons from the institutional failure of high schools, Chapter 1 already documented the vast space between the goal of preparing young people to play meaningful roles in the adult world and the results we are currently producing in urban public high schools. Chapter 2 provided evidence that the American high school was explicitly designed to stratify achievement and that widespread failure served a particular set of historical purposes. Nineteenth-century ideas about intelligence, effort, and merit shaped the selection of students for continued educational opportunity. We are now ready for Step 3 in the process of learning from our failure: drawing upon our best collective wisdom to devise a different approach.

We have learned much in the past several decades to help us rethink our approach to secondary education. Advances in neurobiology, cognitive science, and social psychology give us a much richer understanding of how people learn, why and under what conditions they put in the effort to learn, and when across the lifespan they develop different capacities for learning. We also know that learning can be compromised by psychosocial factors in schools and classrooms that interfere with students' cognitive processes, thwart their intentions, and mask their abilities. The accumulating evidence suggests that ability and effort are not objective indicators of intelligence and character, but rather are socially constructed notions that benefit those with wealth and power.

Unfortunately, our expanding understanding of learning has had little impact on the traditional workings of American high schools; we still operate within an antiquated system designed to churn out winners and losers on the basis of "merit." And not surprisingly, students—particularly low-income students of color—continue to fail at alarming rates. The more we realize how much ability and effort are socially constructed, the more we should question the old ideas about merit that undergird almost everything we do in high school.

WHAT MATTERS FOR MOTIVATION AND LEARNING

Our developing understanding of academic performance suggests that, rather than academic achievement being a function of intelligence and character,

45

it is largely a function of motivation, strategies, and mindsets. As researchers Covington and Teel (1996) summarized, "It is *the reasons that students learn* that largely determine how much they learn, how well they retain knowledge, and whether the knowledge they gain either enhances or detracts from . . . the willingness to learn more" (p. 5, emphasis added). Further, despite accountability pressures that focus almost exclusively on the development of students' content knowledge and skills (what we can call "cognitive factors"), learning depends in large part on *noncognitive* factors—those attitudes, beliefs, and behaviors that contribute to a student's academic success but that aren't directly measured by cognitive tests.

My colleagues and I at the University of Chicago had the opportunity to conduct an extensive review of research on the role of these "noncognitive" factors in student performance (Farrington, Roderick, Allensworth, Nagaoka, Keyes, Johnson, & Beechum, 2012). In reviewing a large body of psychological, economic, and educational literature, we examined five sets of factors—academic behaviors, academic perseverance, academic mindsets, learning strategies, and social skills—and looked at evidence of the relationship of each set of factors to adolescents' course performance. On one hand, we found what you might expect: Academic behaviors such as attending class and doing homework have the most direct relationship to students' grades, and students who show greater academic perseverance—those who put in more "effort" and don't give up easily—earn better grades. This seems entirely consistent with our meritocratic educational system: Hard work pays off. However, the research is also quite clear that academic behaviors and perseverance are closely tied to what students believe about themselves and believe about their ability to learn, and to their access to and use of effective strategies to help them learn. Students with positive academic mindsets and good strategies for learning are most likely to work hard over time and not give up in the face of difficulty, leading them to earn higher grades—regardless of their innate intelligence or prior content knowledge.

Unfortunately, it turns out that social stereotypes and beliefs about intelligence and character give rise to psychological conditions in classrooms that systematically work to the academic benefit of some students and to the detriment of others. As a result, outward manifestations of intelligence and effort—characteristics we thought constituted merit—may instead just be markers of social advantage.

The Powerful Influence of Stereotypes

Anyone who has grown up in the United States has been thoroughly exposed to stereotypes based on race, class, gender, and other social categories. These stereotypes become intertwined with often-subconscious beliefs about character, deficiency, ability, intelligence, motivation, effort, and de-servingness. Even if nobody in a room explicitly endorses offensive stereotypes or beliefs, their power is omnipresent in American life—as Claude Steele (2010) described "floating in the air like a cloud gathering the nation's history" (p. 7).

Everybody knows, for example, the pervasive racial stereotype about Black intellectual inferiority. Awareness of that stereotype is all it takes to interfere with the cognitive functioning and academic performance of African American students (Blascovich, Spencer, Quinn, & Steele, 2001; Schmader & Johns, 2003), so much so that tests and grades systematically underestimate Black students' skills and abilities (Croizet & Dutrévis, 2004; Walton & Spencer, 2009). Likewise, gender stereotypes can directly interfere with girls' and women's cognitive processing while doing math. When viewing MRI images of women's brains as they worked on difficult math problems (and these were women with strong math skills), researchers found that brain activity shifted from the areas normally associated with math processing to the areas associated with social and emotional processing when the subjects were reminded that women are not as good at math as men (Krendl, Richeson, Kelley, & Heatherton, 2008). By activating stereotypes in experimental settings, researchers can systematically lower the cognitive performance of stereotyped groups. In other words, classroom manifestations of "intelligence" may be highly sensitive to context in ways that systematically advantage some students over others.

The good news is that we also have evidence about how to counteract these negative forces and improve classroom performance—even for historically marginalized students. Some of the most exciting psychological research in recent decades shows that when these negative messages are interrupted, student performance significantly increases (Steele, 1997, 2010; Yeager & Walton, 2011). Short-term experiments[1] conducted with middle school, high school, and college-age students demonstrate not only that it is possible to change students' mindsets and neutralize stereotype threats, but that doing so results in students earning higher grades, with the positive effects of these interventions often lasting a year or longer after even the briefest intervention (e.g., Blackwell, Trzeniewski, & Dweck, 2007; Good, Aronson, & Inzlicht, 2003; Oyserman, Terry, & Bybee, 2002; Walton & Cohen, 2007).

Perhaps most important, for our equity and excellence, many of these experimental interventions showed the biggest effects on Black and Latino students (and on girls in math and science classes). Researchers say this is because they intentionally designed experiments to counteract the effects of stereotypes and other negative beliefs floating around in the schooling environment that disproportionately undermine the academic achievement of stereotyped groups (Aronson, Cohen, & McColskey, 2009; Yeager &

Walton, 2011). By neutralizing those messages through their interventions, researchers removed artificial constraints on minority students' performance, and their performance improved.

Academic Mindsets Drive Effort and Perseverance

To better understand how stereotypes affect learning, we need to understand some of the research on academic mindsets. An academic mindset is an attitude or belief students hold about themselves in relation to academic work. Some students bring positive mindsets with them to school—beliefs and attitudes they learned from their families and communities. But mindsets are also significantly shaped by students' schooling experiences and by pervasive messages in society. In our review of the research literature, my colleagues and I focused on four mindsets found to be motivationally very powerful; each of these is briefly explained below. We expressed the four mindsets in the first person from the perspective of the student: "I can succeed at this," "My ability and competence grow with my efforts," "This work has value for me," and "I belong in this academic community" (Farrington et al., 2012). The evidence clearly shows that the more a student endorses any of these beliefs, the more he or she will expend effort to learn. Of course, whether or not a particular mindset seems "believable" to a student depends in large part on conditions within classrooms that structure how learning happens and define opportunities for success or failure. Importantly, unless teachers take intentional actions to equalize motivational conditions in the classroom, mindsets tend to work in favor of the most privileged students and against those who enter school with the least advantage.

"I Can Succeed at This." In order to learn a particular body of knowledge or successfully complete a particular task, we need to believe we can. Human beings—adults and children alike—put forth effort where we think it will pay (Bandura, 1986). It's not surprising, then, that a distinguished panel of research scientists concluded that increasing student motivation in the classroom largely depended on "creat[ing] a set of circumstances in which students . . . come to believe that . . . they can reasonably expect to be able to learn the material" (National Research Council and the Institute of Medicine, 2004). The classroom circumstances surrounding an academic task are particularly important because students' expectations for success are less determined by how much ability they actually have or how hard the material really is than by students' *perceptions* of themselves and of the academic task.

A student's perception that she will succeed at a specific task or in a specific classroom (known as an efficacy belief) directly affects how long she will stick to a difficult task and how she will respond to setbacks (Pajares,

1996). Not surprisingly, people won't put much persistent effort into something if they don't expect to be successful (Oyserman & James, 2009). In this way, efficacy beliefs trump actual skills. Regardless of their objective ability to successfully complete a task, students are much quicker to give up if they don't believe they can do it. Conversely, students with questionable skills will nonetheless show high levels of effort, perseverance, *and success* if they believe they can accomplish a learning goal (Bandura, 1986; Bandura & Schunk, 1981; Bouffard-Bouchard, 1990; Lent, Brown, & Larkin, 1984; Pajares, 1996; Schunk & Hanson, 1985).

Upper-income, White, or Asian students tend to be surrounded by messages about their academic prowess. They are more likely to go to high-performing high schools, more likely to be in the top academic track, more likely to take advanced coursework, more likely to earn high grades, and more likely to graduate from high school and college than low-income, Black, or Latino students. They are more likely to have parents who went to college, and hence are more likely to see tangible evidence of the connection between school performance and their future options. Everything around them reinforces the notion that "I can succeed at this." This is not to say that young people in this position have it easy. The performance pressures on privileged students can be enormous, largely because everybody expects them to do well. They are surrounded by evidence of and expectation for their likely success in school.

Meanwhile, low-income African American and Latino students in urban districts commonly attend what are universally understood to be "low-performing" or "failing" schools—known as such due to the poor academic performance of the students who attend them. If they go to schools with Whites and Asians, Black and Latino students are most likely to be in the lowest-tracked classes. Because of federal accountability policies under No Child Left Behind, minority students now in high school have spent all of their schooling lives under a cloud of social anxiety about achievement gaps and low test scores. Everybody knows that, on average, Black and Latino students perform poorly on standardized tests compared with Whites and Asians. Everybody knows that Black and Latino males are the most likely of any group to drop out of high school. These "facts" send powerful messages to the least advantaged students about their likelihood to succeed in school. Every time Black and Latino kids get a low grade or yet another standardized test result showing how poorly they did compared with other students in the state, it undermines their ability to believe they can succeed, making them less likely to put forth effort on future academic tasks.

"My Ability and Competence Grow with My Effort." In addition to students' beliefs about their likelihood of success, students benefit by believing they can increase their academic ability by trying hard. Students with a "growth mindset" believe that working hard will make them smarter (Dweck, 2006). They are motivated toward mastery. If they do poorly on a piece of schoolwork, they interpret that as a sign that they didn't try hard enough and respond with increased effort (Cury, Elliott, Da Fonseca, & Moller, 2006; Dweck & Leggett, 1988). Conversely, students with a "fixed mindset" believe that their school performance is determined by their level of intelligence and is something they cannot change. They interpret academic difficulty as a sign that they are not smart enough, so they tend to give up easily when work gets hard (Kelley, 1973; Vispoel & Austin, 1995; Weiner, 1986). Notably, across a large number of studies, students' beliefs about intelligence and their attributions for academic success or failure were more strongly associated with their school performance than was their actual measured ability (i.e., test scores). In other words, whether a student believes intelligence is fixed or believes it can grow with effort is more predictive of success than *how much* intelligence he or she has.

"This Work Has Value for Me." A third academic mindset has to do with the value students place on the work they are doing. Human beings are naturally motivated to learn when we find something to be inherently interesting or valuable (Bruner, 1960; McCombs, 1991, 1993, 1994). The more students see a connection between schoolwork and their own interests, lives, or futures, the more likely they are to engage in school tasks, the longer they will persist at doing those tasks, and the better their performance will be (Atkinson, 1957; Damon, 2008; Eccles, Adler, Futterman, Goff, Kaczala, Meece, & Midgley, 1983; McKnight & Kashdan, 2009; Wigfield, 1994; Wigfield & Eccles, 1992). In this case, interest trumps ability in determining school performance.

Unfortunately, across all racial groups, academic interest wanes as students move from elementary school to the middle grades to high school (Marks, 2000). In the absence of natural interest in academic studies, high school students often struggle to apply themselves to their work. For students who don't see connections between what they do in school and what they really care about, or who cannot easily envision a future for themselves in college or career, maintaining focus on school tasks can require more effort than students can muster. Even when students *do* try to focus on something that is inherently uninteresting to them, they are likely to experience mental fatigue, interfering with their ability to learn (Kaplan & Kaplan, 1982). It turns out the human brain is physically incapable of paying attention to something that is uninteresting for prolonged periods of time. If students have to expend mental energy trying to focus, they have less mental energy available for processing information and learning. Regardless of how smart students are or how hard they try, being bored places a real limit on their ability to think.

Helping students see how academic work is related to things they care about has a very positive effect on school performance. Students from more privileged backgrounds are more likely to see themselves going to college or having careers related to their academic work, and thus can more readily see connections between school and their futures. They are likely to have broader background knowledge, helping them place their learning in a larger (and more interesting) context. This gives them a further psychological and performance advantage over students who struggle to see the relevance of their studies.

"I Belong in This Academic Community." The fourth academic mindset my colleagues and I explored in our research review focused on students' sense of belonging. Young people are much more strongly motivated to participate in academic activities if they feel themselves to be full members of a school or classroom community that collectively values learning (Battistich, Solomon, Kim, Watson, & Schaps, 1995; Cohen & Garcia, 2008; Furrer & Skinner, 2003; Goodenow & Grady, 1993; McMillan & Chavis, 1986; Solomon, Watson, Battistich, Schaps, & Delucchi; 1996; Wentzel & Caldwell, 1997). In an extensive review of the research on school belonging, Osterman (2000) concludes that:

> The experience of belongingness is associated with important psychological processes. Children who experience a sense of relatedness [in school] . . . perceive themselves to be more competent and autonomous and have higher levels of intrinsic motivation [than students with a low sense of belonging]. . . . These inner resources in turn predict engagement and performance. . . . [Students who experience belonging] have more positive attitudes toward school, classwork, teachers, and their peers. . . . They invest more of themselves in the learning process. (p. 343)

On the other hand, "rejection or the sense of exclusion or estrangement from the group is consistently associated with behavioral problems in the classroom (either aggression or withdrawal), lower interest in school, lower achievement, and dropout" (p. 343).

In short, students are more motivated and will expend more effort to learn if their natural need for belonging is being met at school. The research strongly suggests that racial/ethnic and gender stereotypes in the larger social environment undermine the sense of belonging of minority students, who often feel they don't fit in academically or socially. This may be particularly true for academically successful students who advance through the ranks (in higher-level courses or in more elite institutions) and find themselves increasingly surrounded by people who do not look like they do.

Theresa Perry and colleagues (2003) emphasize the importance of creating "counter-narratives" of achievement for African American students who have spent most of their school lives being bombarded with negative images and stereotypes about their intellectual deficiency and underperformance. Contending with those images and stereotypes binds up students' mental energy in the classroom. Teachers can counteract negative stereotypes by explicitly tying academic achievement to the social identities of students in the room. By providing students with different frames of reference to interpret their experience in school—by creating inclusive communities where "people like me" are academic achievers—teachers can free up a lot more student energy for learning.

Learning Strategies Enable Success

In addition to academic mindsets, we also found considerable evidence of the importance of learning strategies to school performance. The old view of student learning was that students mastered academic content through innate intelligence and sheer effort. What we now understand is that the best learners are *strategic*, meaning that successful students use strategies to manage the tasks of learning. Accomplished students think about what a task is asking them to do, devise a plan of action, estimate how much time and effort the task will take, monitor what happens as they embark on their learning plan, notice when they hit a wall or something they weren't expecting, diagnose every problem or setback that arises, come up with a new strategy to move forward, check to see if that strategy is working, and continue this process until their learning goal is met (National Research Council, 2002). They can also tell when they have arrived at understanding, so they don't keep going past the point they tried to reach, and they also don't stop before they arrive. All of these are examples of learning strategies that are essential to developing deep understanding. Students who use these strategies (sometimes consciously and intentionally, sometimes automatically without their awareness) have much stronger academic performance than students who don't (Garner & Alexander, 1989; Schoenfeld, 1987). In the absence of effective learning strategies, even students with high intellectual ability who put in lots of effort may look like they don't know what they are doing.

Learning strategies can be effectively taught and learned in the context of regular classroom instruction (Collins & Smith, 1982; Lester, Masingila, Mau, Lambdin, dos Santon, & Raymond, 1994; National Research Council, 2012; Schoenfeld, 1983, 1985). Teachers help students become more strategic learners by modeling their own use of effective strategies and by making explicit their thinking as they approach questions or encounter problems while engaging with students in intellectual work.

Unfortunately, whether or not students get access to learning strategies seems to differ by race and class. Oyserman (2008) asserted that youth in "under-resourced contexts" may desire to do well in school and may perceive school success as important, but they are less likely to learn effective academic strategies than students in homes and schools with more resources. In the absence of concrete strategies, "youth may maintain an abstract commitment to education" without this translating into behaviors that bring success (p. 274). Higher-income students (disproportionately White or Asian) are more likely to be given cues for positive academic behaviors in their schools, homes, peer groups, and larger social environments and are more likely to be assisted by others around them when they encounter academic difficulties (e.g., provided with private tutors, assisted with homework, protected from encroachments on study time at home). Low-income students (disproportionately African American or Latino) often have to rely on developing their own strategies for success (Oyserman, Terry, & Bybee, 2002). Having access to concrete academic strategies also reinforces motivation and feelings of self-efficacy. Students are more likely to believe they can succeed when they know they have effective tools to improve their school performance. Here again, however, students who enter school with social advantages also have more access to effective learning strategies, making them look smarter and more hardworking than students who don't have access to these tools.

Adolescent Identities Affect School Performance

To better understand why academic mindsets are so powerful—and why students with greater social advantage are likely to benefit from more positive mindsets—let's look at what we have come to understand over the past several decades about the development of adolescent identities. Note that I say here adolescent "identities"—plural. We like to believe that our identity stays fairly constant from minute to minute—the "self" as a relatively stable entity (Swann, 1997)—but psychological research shows that self-concept is highly malleable and sensitive to external cues (Markus & Kunda, 1986). In other words, how we experience ourselves changes in response to where we are and whom we are with. Different contexts can cue different parts of a person's self-concept, often simultaneously (Oyserman, 2001).

Consider the young person who is a teenager, female, African American, a student, a clarinet player, a runner, from a working-class family, part of this group of friends, in a specific neighborhood, in a particular city. Each of these contexts sends messages to the student about who she is, how she ought to behave, and what she is capable of. When these messages are consistent with one another, the task of developing a coherent sense of self is fairly straightforward. But to the extent that these socially cued messages "are contradictory, grounded in different assumptions, or irrelevant to one another, a person is faced with a more complex and effortful self-construction and maintenance task" (Oyserman & Markus, 1998, p. 120). Put simply, it's a lot easier to be a good student when being a good student is consistent with other identities that are important to us. Conflicts between students' academic identities and social identities can derail their success in school and complicate their attempts to improve their academic performance.

Students draw upon frames of reference they share with important social groups to determine how to act and "who to be" in school affecting their academic performance. Social context works powerfully with students' social identities to both define and constrain their sense of what is possible for them. To the extent that we value membership in our important social groups, "we can become the kind of person that people of our group can become [and] we fear disappointing important groups by failing to attain group norms and standards" (Oyserman & Fryberg, 2006, p. 21).

Students' social identities affect their sense of "how high to aim" in terms of educational performance and attainment, based on group norms (Harvey & Schroder, 1963). A failing student will likely receive conflicting messages from different social groups about what he ought to have expected of himself. The strength of his identification with one group over another will shape his interpretations of academic failure. Which of the images he holds of himself is "most true": the son in a family that holds high expectations for his behavior or the fun-loving guy in his relatively low-performing peer group? Some researchers complicate this picture further, noting that academic achievement for minority students often comes at a significant personal price. If we define academic success according to narrow, dominant-cultural images of intellectual achievement, we may inadvertently force students from other cultures to choose between conflicting notions of success (Espinoza-Herold, 2003).

Language plays a central role in this conundrum. Students face particular challenges in developing a strong academic identity if the language associated with academic success is in conflict with language that reaffirms their cultural identity or deepens their relationships with friends. Labov (1982) noted that language patterns that strengthened social relations among low-income African American students also served to alienate them from White teachers who viewed such language as defiant. If students spoke "school English" to comply with teachers' wishes, they might smooth their path to academic success and make themselves appear more "deserving" of the teacher's effort and attention, but they risked social rejection by stepping outside the shared linguistic code of their Black peer culture. Faced with the choice between peer acceptance and academic success, students of color might adopt speech patterns that successfully cement peer relationships but that undermine relationships with teachers and increase the possibility of academic failure. White, middle-class students experience no such conflicts in the classroom, as "school English" tends to be their home language.

In addition to peer influences on adolescent identities, teenagers also hit important developmental milestones as they enter high school. They become more aware of the temporal quality of the self. A girl in early adolescence comes to recognize in a deeper way that different versions of herself existed in the past, she is her own particular self now, and she will be different in the future. This temporal dimension again points to both the stability ("I am always me") and the malleability ("I am changing and growing") of the self. With awareness of temporality is an understanding that choices one makes and actions one takes now will affect who one will be in the future. Making and acting upon decisions about one's future self is a fundamental task of adolescence—though students are just beginning to learn how to do this when they enter high school.

Daphna Oyserman and her colleagues use the concept of "possible selves" to describe potential future versions of oneself (Oyserman, Terry, & Bybee, 2002), asserting that students are most likely to regulate their academic behavior when certain conditions are in place. First, they can envision positive and negative versions of their possible selves, both "what a person hopes to become [and what a person] fears that he or she might become" (Oyserman & Markus, 1990, p. 141). To affect behavior, however, adolescents also need strategies to bring about desired future selves as well as strategies for avoiding negative future selves (Oyserman, Terry, & Bybee, 2002). Finally, these possible selves and related strategies must not conflict with students' important social identities (Oyserman & James, 2009).

The identity development task of adolescents is a complicated process, particularly if there is nothing in place in schools to interrupt negative racial/ethnic stereotypes. Oyserman, Terry, and Bybee (2002) noted that "low income African American youth may find it difficult to create positive and believable possible selves focused on school as a pathway to adulthood unless these possible selves are fostered in a social context" that connects being a high-achieving student with being African American (p. 314). In an experiment to help African American middle school students in Detroit develop future possible selves and strategies to attain them, researchers found that these students were more bonded to school, cared more about doing well, improved their attendance, and (for boys) got in less trouble than students in a matched control group (Oyserman, Terry, & Bybee, 2002). Key to these results was connecting academic achievement to students' African American racial identity.[2]

THE TEACHER'S CONUNDRUM

The psychological research presents a different picture from the one painted by our antiquated notions of intelligence, character, effort, and merit. In recent decades, we have come to understand learning to be a complex sociocultural phenomenon, a dynamic process strongly shaped by one's beliefs, self-concept, past experience, social interactions, and the context in which one is trying to learn. To the extent that pervasive historical, socioeconomic, and cultural forces have different effects on young people growing up in the United States depending on their race, ethnicity, class, gender, language, or other particulars of their unique identities, we could also expect them to have very different experiences of, beliefs about, and dispositions toward learning.

More to the point, we could expect that some students would enjoy a particular configuration of experiences that strongly supported their ability to learn. A world that affirms young people's capabilities, that provides opportunities to develop their potential and to experience their competence, that assumes they will perform well academically, that promises a productive future and introduces students to role models just like them, that draws on examples they understand and uses words they hear at home—all of these things support young people's ability and likelihood to successfully engage in learning. Under these circumstances, students are much more likely to work hard at school and demonstrate what look like high levels of academic ability and motivation (intelligence and effort).

Meanwhile, other students may experience something very different. If students worry that their teachers doubt their ability to do the assigned work, if teachers are anxious about students' test scores and seem to grow frustrated by students' questions, if students' parents have limited formal education themselves and little familiarity with advanced academic coursework, if their textbooks are full of references to things they've never heard of, if their school is labeled as failing due to the collective performance of their peers, if all the images young people see of professional adults don't look like anyone in their neighborhood, if they are bombarded by stereotypes depicting them as stupid or lazy, students' ability to engage in learning becomes seriously compromised, despite how smart they are or how much they care. Under these circumstances, students are likely to be easily frustrated at school, withdraw their efforts, and demonstrate what looks like indifference or limited intellectual capacity.

The extensive body of research on the psychological prerequisites to academic achievement presents a conundrum for teachers in a system built on deservingness and merit. We have always known that resources are inequitably distributed in our society and that differences in the quality of students' schooling experiences must contribute to differences in their academic outcomes. But we have also clung to the belief that we could fairly assess students' academic performance, in large part because we have continued to believe that academic performance ultimately really does come down to ability and effort. I don't know a single teacher who would say he or she gave out grades—and especially failing grades—that a student did not deserve. Within our own classrooms, where we work hard to provide everyone with equal opportunity, where we set up systems to help students succeed, where we strive for fairness and objectivity in our grading of student work, we have to believe that students' ability and effort ultimately account for the differences we see in their performance.

Research on academic mindsets and learning strategies fundamentally challenges this assumption. The idea that motivated students deserve to succeed and unmotivated students deserve to fail gives way to a different set of ideas: that student motivation and effort are socially constructed in ways that benefit students with more status and privilege, and that schools systematically reinforce this construction. Although humans do differ in their levels of innate intelligence, differences in intelligence barely begin to account for differences in academic performance. Intellectually capable students may be prevented from more successfully engaging in and completing academic tasks if they lack effective learning strategies. Negative academic mindsets and other psychosocial factors in schools and classrooms can actually suppress students' cognitive functioning. On the hopeful side, schools could construct motivation differently to benefit a much broader range of students. Collectively, the research on human learning suggests not only that there is huge untapped potential in American classrooms, but that perhaps almost anybody could learn almost anything, given sufficient time and the right conditions. If only our high schools were organized for this purpose.

Part II

STUDYING FAILURE

There is absolutely no inevitability as long as there is a willingness to contemplate what is happening.

—Marshall McLuhan

FOUR

Looking Closely at Failure

Fourteen Students in Three Urban High Schools

Education research has done an impressive job describing a host of factors contributing to high school dropout and the costs to youth and society of students who leave school without diplomas. Surprisingly few of these studies actually involved talking to kids. To better understand widespread academic failure in urban high schools, I decided to talk with students who knew it first-hand. This chapter describes two qualitative studies I conducted to shed light on structural and psychological mechanisms and processes that perpetuate student failure. I wanted to know what students would say about failure, and how structural and psychological features that were implicated in history and research—reviewed in Chapters 1–3—might shape students' beliefs about their ability, sense of belonging, or understanding of themselves as learners. By following the trail of failing grades, I hoped to better understand *why* 9th-grade course failure so accurately predicts who will drop out of high school.

STUDY 1: A PILOT STUDY OF STUDENTS' EXPERIENCES OF FAILURE

In 2007 I interviewed six students in their second year of high school as part of a small, exploratory study. Each student had failed two or more freshman courses, statistically putting them at great risk for dropping out of school. My pilot study was guided by two questions: (1) Why do so few students recover once they start failing classes? (2) Is there something about the ma-chinery of failure in traditional high schools (grades, credits, credit recovery systems, penalties, and supports) that undermines students' chances of re-covering once they start to fail? In interviews, I asked students about their grades, credits, feelings about success and failure, and plans for getting back on track toward graduation. However, to really understand if traditional grading and credit structures had any impact on student failure, I needed a counterfactual, some point of comparison. My premise was that traditional high school structures—seat time, grades, and Carnegie units—were chiefly responsible for the long-term negative consequences of course failure. But maybe it was the *act* of failing itself that created long-term consequences, rather than the particular way failing was structured. To test my hypothesis, I needed to find a school that somehow structured failure differently.

At that time, Chicago was in the midst of its "Renaissance 2010" initiative: a plan announced in 2004 by then-Mayor Richard M. Daley to open 100 new public schools by the year 2010. The stated rationale for Renaissance 2010 was to encourage innovation and increase high-quality educational options for Chicago families in the public school system. Renaissance 2010 schools included new, small "conversion" high schools that replaced some large, low-performing neighborhood schools; public charter schools; and other district-run new schools.

One of the new small charter schools—"Devon High School" (a pseudonym)—used the leeway granted in its charter to conduct an experiment. Devon teachers and administrators thought the downward spiral of student failure and dropout might be interrupted by providing clear mechanisms to help students recover from failure. To this end, Devon High changed the way students were graded and earned course credit.[1] Devon implemented a competency-based assessment system, evaluating students on their mastery of learning outcomes specified for each course, using ratings of *Proficient (P)*, *High Performance (HP)*, or *Not Yet Proficient (NY)* to describe student performance on each outcome. Students passed classes and earned course credit by demonstrating proficiency (a rating of *P* or *HP*) in course outcomes. Devon students could "fail" a class and hence fail to earn course credit, but rather than taking a failed class all over again from the beginning, students essentially got an "incomplete" until they did additional work and demonstrated proficiency in unmet learning outcomes, and thereby earned course credit.

Devon's alternative grading and credit structure allowed me to compare the experience of student failure in the traditional system with that of student failure in this alternative system. In Study 1, three students attended "Maxwell High" (again, a pseudonym), a traditional neighborhood high school, and three students attended Devon High, the public charter school with the alternative grading system. (Profiles of these schools appear later in the chapter.)

I interviewed each of these six students once in spring 2007 and was granted access to their 9th-grade academic records. Two preliminary themes emerged from my interviews. The first was a common rhetoric of hope among all the students. Apparently unaware of the dim statistical likelihood that they would finish high school, all six students were determined to make up missing credits and graduate with their peers.

However, for students at Maxwell (the traditional high school), this hope for the future was coupled with a sense of futility in the present. Even as they laid out plans to recover credits and get back on track to graduate, all three Maxwell students were failing at least one current class and expressed little hope of being able to finish the semester without accumulating more Fs. This contrasted with the beliefs of Devon (charter school) students, who all expressed confidence they would pass their current classes, even those they were failing at the time of the interviews. When I asked about reasons for their optimism, Devon students each mentioned specific school policies and practices that would facilitate their success. I share excerpts from these student interviews in Chapters 5 through 8.

The second key theme, expressed by all six students, was a pervasive sense of personal responsibility for their academic successes or failures. Every student said it was "up to me" to get serious about school and pass classes. They believed academic achievement was an entirely individual accomplishment.

However, students at Maxwell seemed to experience this responsibility as a particularly lonely venture. They felt little support from adults in school and had no clear strategies to improve their academic performance. Maxwell students often voiced their belief that the way to recover from their precarious academic status was simply to "try harder." Devon students, in contrast, pointed to school policies and practices that would support them. While affirming that it was personally up to them to work harder and pass classes, Devon students also expressed confidence that there were people to help them and structures in place, as part of their school's alternative grading system, to support their success. Figure 4.1 illustrates the picture that started to emerge from Study 1 of the process whereby failure affects students' future academic performance.

My preliminary findings raised questions about why students experienced some school policies and practices as being supportive and effective, while other school policies and practices were not recognized, were not experienced as a support, or were perceived as actually constraining students' quest for academic success. How did different school policies and practices influence the effects of initial course failure on students' subsequent academic performance? How did these policies and practices contribute to how students made sense of and responded to academic failure? What happened in classrooms and in students' interactions with teachers that might influence students' beliefs about their own abilities or their chances of success? Questions raised by these initial interviews were the impetus for Study 2—my dissertation research—the following year.

Figure 4.1. Student Experience, Sensemaking, Responses, and Outcomes

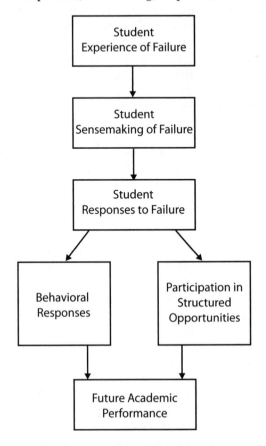

STUDY 2: HOW CLASSROOMS
AND SCHOOLS SHAPE STUDENT FAILURE

In 2008, I conducted a more in-depth study of failing students, their class-rooms, and their schools. I used a "sensemaking" framework in Study 2 designed around this central idea: When students fail classes, they draw on their environment to make sense of that failure—to decide what failure means about who they are and what they are doing—and to decide how to behave in response. Sensemaking involves both psychological and structural elements. School and classroom structures, policies, and practices shape the context and circumstances that lead to failure, shape students' immediate environment for "explaining" failure, and also shape students' potential response options.

I was interested in students' opportunities for both *remediation* and *recovery*. A student who fails a class is doubly hurt: (1) academically, she has not sufficiently mastered the knowledge and skills taught in the class that she will ostensibly need in the future; and (2) structurally, she is short on credits to advance toward graduation. To pull herself out of failure and make progress toward a diploma, she needs opportunities both to remediate her learning—i.e., learn the material she previously failed to master—and to recover her lost credits. In Study 2, I sought to understand the extent to which failing students had access to opportunities for remediation and recovery, how much students availed themselves of these opportunities, and what happened when they did or they didn't.

Drawing on what I learned about the history of high schools, I entered Study 2 (my dissertation research) with a hypothesis: that the constellation of structures, policies, and practices around student failure in a given high school would either function to promote *selection and stratification*, acting as *constraints* on failing students and limiting their access to opportunities, or they would function to promote *equity and excellence* by acting as *supports* to failing students and mobilizing resources for student success. As in my pilot study, this all begged a corollary question: If failure in a given school served a different function from its historical selection and stratification function, i.e., if a school and its classrooms were designed to fulfill an equity and excellence function, would these structural differences affect how students experienced failure and how they acted in response to it? If indeed the approaches of different schools led to different student experiences of and responses to failure, how might these differences affect students' subsequent academic performance, and hence their likelihood of graduation? As in Study 1, this necessitated a comparison between the policies and practices of two schools with differing orientations toward student failure.

To explore these questions, I added onto my initial model of student sensemaking. In Study 2, I embedded students' sensemaking and response processes in classrooms and schools (and ultimately in a larger social context), as illustrated in Figure 4.2. I reasoned that students' experiences of failure, sensemaking about failure, and responses to failure would all be affected directly by classrooms, through individual teachers' grading policies and instructional practices. They would also be affected directly by their school, through structural mechanisms such as the way the year is divided into marking periods, the school's overall grading and credit system, and available opportunities for students to remediate learning and recover credits. Schools also would have indirect effects on student failure through classrooms, by shaping or mandating certain classroom policies and practices and influencing the ways teachers teach and evaluate students. Lastly, schools, classrooms, and students themselves would interpret larger social messages about the meanings of failure, the value of a high school diploma, the purposes of education, and their own chances of success, either directly or indirectly affecting students' interpretations of and responses to failure. Figure 4.2 depicts these hypothesized relationships and effects.

For Study 2, I used a comparative case study design, with eight student cases. In spring 2008, I went back to Devon High to talk with five more students there. I also interviewed three students at "Alexander High School" (a pseudonym), another of the new small schools opened in Chicago under Renaissance 2010.[2] Each student participated in two in-depth interviews in spring, once around the time of third-quarter report cards and again in the last month of school. In this expanded study, I also wanted to understand how classrooms and schools affected students' sense of failure and response to failure. In addition to interviewing students, then, I collected data about their schools and classrooms through observations and interviews with teachers, principals, and counselors. Table 4.1 lists the number of participants in Study 2 and the kinds of evidence I collected.

In interviewing students about their failure experiences, I was not trying to gather objective facts. (I already had students' transcripts, so I knew

Figure 4.2. Student Sensemaking of Failure in Classrooms and Schools

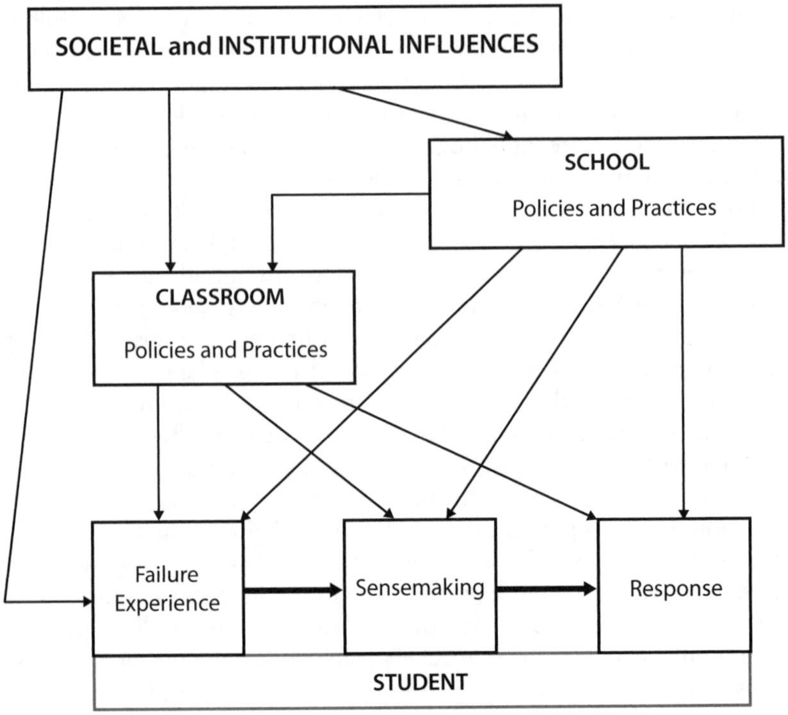

Table 4.1. Study 2 Participants and Types of Evidence

Types of Evidence	Data on Students	Data on Classrooms	Data on Schools
Student Interviews	8 students (3 at Alexander, 5 at Devon)	8 students (3 at Alexander, 5 at Devon)	8 students (3 at Alexander, 5 at Devon)
School/Classroom Observations	11 classroom observations (4 at Alexander, 7 at Devon)	11 classroom observations (4 at Alexander, 7 at Devon)	4 school observations (2 at each school)
Teacher Interviews		10 teachers (3 at Alexander, 7 at Devon)	10 teachers (3 at Alexander, 7 at Devon)
Administrator Interviews			4 administrators (2 at Alexander, 2 at Devon)
Documentary Evidence	Students' academic high school records		School policies, handbooks, announcements

their grades in each class.) Rather, I wanted to understand the perceptions and interpretations of students grappling with the meaning of course failure in light of their developing identities and in the context of their goals for the future.

THREE URBAN AMERICAN HIGH SCHOOLS TRYING TO GET IT RIGHT

Urban high schools are fraught with failures of all kinds. In studying the structures of academic failure in both Study 1 and Study 2, I chose schools that were relatively high-functioning organizations compared with many of their peer institutions. Though all three schools were on "academic warning" for low test scores and had few students meeting state standards—similar to most high schools in Chicago—Maxwell, Devon, and Alexander High Schools each had visionary, competent leaders and hard-working, dedicated teachers. Each school was making significant efforts to increase student learning, to raise graduation rates, and to increase college enrollment rates. All three schools enrolled over 90% minority students and served predominantly low-income families. By focusing on relatively well-organized but struggling urban schools, I hoped to eliminate from consideration the most egregious school-level problems that might explain high urban failure rates. In high schools that were basically working hard to do things right but serving a population with myriad challenges, how did the traditional construction of failure function?

Maxwell High School, a Traditional Neighborhood School (Study 1)

Maxwell High was a longstanding Chicago high school, a neighborhood institution. Though the school was located in a racially integrated area, few White students attended the school. In 2007, 93% of Maxwell's 1,800 students were African American (the remaining 7% included Asian, Latino, and White students) and 70% of students qualified for the federal free or reduced lunch program. Maxwell students scored higher than the district average on statewide achievement tests, with 40% of students meeting Illinois State Standards in 2007. This was due in part to special magnet programs that attracted a small number of higher-achieving students to Maxwell's top academic track. Still, fewer than 3% of the student body exceeded state standards in any subject in 2007. That year, the school had a 5-year graduation rate of 72%, significantly higher than the district average. Maxwell High School's mission statement focused on "college success," and its visionary young African American principal worked hard to instill a college-going culture throughout the school. One in six students at Maxwell took Advanced Placement classes in 2007, though the AP exam pass rate (score of 3 or higher) was only 25%. Overall, Maxwell was a school striving to better serve neighborhood families and better prepare its students for college.

Meanwhile, a significant number of Maxwell students failed classes. Despite the efforts of its dynamic principal, the school struggled against institutional inertia, and tradition often dictated its response to student failure. According to district statistics, 34% of Maxwell freshmen were "off track" at the end of 9th grade in 2007, meaning one in three freshmen failed two or more core semester courses or earned fewer than 5 credits by the end of their first year. Mediocre attendance interfered with student success. Maxwell had an overall daily attendance rate just below 88%, with one in three students classified as a chronic truant. Although school administrators recognized problems with attendance and freshman course failure and were taking steps to address these issues, their energy and focus were divided between increasing academic rigor for higher-achieving students and ameliorating failure among struggling students. In this regard, Maxwell was a very traditional neighborhood high school and typical of many large urban public schools across the country.

Alexander High School, a New Small School (Study 2)

Alexander High was one of several new small schools opened under Chicago's Renaissance 2010 initiative.[3] The district closed an old vocational high school in this low-income, African American neighborhood, citing dwindling enrollment and low test scores. The surrounding community had suffered decades of disinvestment and was notorious for problems with gangs, drugs, and violent crime. Community leaders welcomed the new small school on the old vocational campus, hoping it would improve educational opportunities for neighborhood youth. The school advertised itself as providing a "safer, more productive learning environment" by virtue of its small size. In my interviews, safety was one of the features Alexander students reported most appreciating about the school.

Alexander High was started by a group of union teachers from another CPS high school. One of its founding teachers, a skillful, young African American woman, was elected as principal and still served in that capacity at the time of my study. Although the school was managed by the district, Alexander utilized a "teacher-led" governance structure within the school itself, with teachers collectively addressing problems and routinely setting policy within the parameters allowed by the city school board and its own local school council. On average, the 35 teachers at Alexander had over 13 years of classroom experience. By and large each had made a conscious choice to teach at Alexander and was committed to serving its student population, which was 99% African American and 90% low-income.

In 2008, approximately 550 students were enrolled at Alexander in grades 9 through 12. Admission was open to all city residents, though the school reserved the majority of enrollment slots for neighborhood students. Alexander admitted 140 students into 9th grade each year without regard to test scores or other performance criteria. Applications exceeded available slots every year, so admissions were decided by lottery, and the school maintained a waiting list.

The mission of Alexander High School was to "inspire students to intellectual excellence" and community activism. Alexander was explicitly a "college-preparatory" school, and teachers and administrators were actively engaged in creating a college-going culture in the building. Its website affirmed the belief that all Alexander students "can graduate and go on to college" and stated that students would be "immersed in a culture of achievement and high expectations."

Alexander High School held its first graduation ceremony in June 2008. A full 84% of the 140 students who entered Alexander in 2004 graduated within 4 years (compared with the districtwide 4-year graduation rate of 53%). Clearly, the school's strategies for motivating and supporting academic achievement seemed to be working. All 117 of its graduates were accepted into college in 2004, and over 60% of those students enrolled within a year of graduating from high school.

These graduation data were particularly impressive because Alexander was serving a student population for whom academic excellence and college-going were not the norm. Alexander students struggled to perform well on state standardized tests. Only 15% of 11th-graders met or exceeded state standards in 2007, compared with the district average of 30% and statewide average of 53%. Alexander espoused a "constructivist" approach to teaching and learning and promoted the use of "project-based inquiry," although the principal said she struggled to make this part of regular teacher practice, with many teachers displaying greater comfort with more traditional instructional methods. Though its students were lower-performing than students at Maxwell High, 75% of Alexander students were on track to graduate at the end of freshman year, a rate surpassing Maxwell's. Alexander's teachers were paying close attention to student failure rates and were actively trying to support student achievement.

In short, Alexander was a small urban school serving a population of low-income African American students who, as a whole, struggled academically. Alexander's teachers and administrators were determinedly focused on preparing students for college, which they saw as a battle of both "hearts and minds." The school was imbued with a college-going culture and a focus on academics, evidenced everywhere within the school building. As such, Alexander was similar to many new small schools opened in urban districts in the past 10 or 20 years.

Devon High School, a Small Charter School (Study 1 and Study 2)

As I described earlier, I selected Devon High School for inclusion in both my pilot study and dissertation study because of its alternative grading and credit system. Devon provided a rare and important contrast to schools using traditional methods of evaluating, promoting, and passing or failing students. Another significant feature of Devon was that it was an all-girls school, founded to increase the number of low-income women of color in math, science, and engineering. As a result, much of my work in collecting and analyzing data focused on disentangling the effects of Devon's single-sex environment from the effects of the school's alternative approach to student evaluation. Because Devon enrolled only young women, in Study 2 I limited my sample to young women at Alexander High as well. (Study 1 included girls at Devon and both boys and girls at Maxwell High.)

At the time I began collecting data, Devon was a relatively new high school (the Class of 2007 was its fourth graduating class) and had no particular legacy to uphold, giving the school more freedom to create its own culture. Devon was also much smaller than a typical neighborhood school, enrolling just under 350 students in grades 7 through 12. As a charter school, it drew from a wide geographical area of the city. In 2007, the student population at Devon was 100% female, 74% African American, 13% Latina, 7% White, 5% multiethnic, and 1% Asian. Approximately 81% of Devon students qualified for free or reduced lunch. The school admitted 75 students into 9th grade each year, over half of whom came from its own middle school. Its admissions criteria and enrollment lottery were the same as Alexander's, except that it did not set aside slots for neighborhood residents. Like Alexander, Devon maintained a waiting list every year.

Devon was led by a highly experienced principal, an older White woman who formerly taught high school math and earned her PhD in math education. The school had 29 teachers on staff and a distributed leadership approach to decision making. Like the faculty at Alexander, most of Devon's teachers were committed to social justice pedagogy and felt fully committed to the school's mission of "inspiring urban girls to engage in rigorous college preparatory learning . . . that nurtures their self-confidence and challenges them to achieve."

Devon shared another similarity with Alexander in that, despite its emphasis on academic achievement and college preparation, its students did not perform well on standardized tests. In 2007, 17% of Devon's juniors met or exceeded state standards, a rate similar to Alexander's students. Like Alexander, Devon High's graduation rates were significantly more impressive than were its test scores. Devon graduated an average of approximately 70% of students each year, as compared with the district's 53% average. The vast majority of Devon graduates (over 90%) enrolled in college, consistently giving the school one of the highest college enrollment rates of nonselective schools in the city.

Devon was a charter school with significant autonomy, able to implement policies and practices that differed markedly from those in regular district-administered schools. The educators who opened the school were guided by a philosophical commitment to equity and democracy, and to this end intentionally designed a competency-based assessment system to both maximize student learning and minimize student failure. As such, Devon provided a good comparative context for exploring whether students made sense of failure differently in a school that consciously reoriented its grading and credit policies and practices to align with an equity and excellence goal.

FOURTEEN STUDENTS CONTENDING WITH FAILURE

In summary, the three schools—Maxwell, Alexander, and Devon—represented a collection of high schools fairly typical of what one might find in most large cities today: a larger traditional neighborhood high school, a new small school opened on the campus of a closed vocational school, and a small charter school. They ranged in size from 350 to 1,800 students. The youth they served were similar in many respects across schools, mostly low-income and African American, although Maxwell had slightly more middle- and high-achieving students than the other two schools, and Devon was a single-sex school serving young women. In a racially segregated city, these three schools looked very much like other Chicago schools in African American neighborhoods on the south and west sides of the city. The salient distinguishing feature among them was Devon's alternative assessment system, an approach to grading that sought to redefine student failure and its consequences.

The six students in Study 1 and eight students in Study 2 were all in their second year of high school when I interviewed them. As a result of course failures and subsequent credit deficiency, all 14 students were part of the "9th-grade bubble" discussed in Chapter 1: 2 years into high school but technically considered freshmen. As reviewed earlier, research in Chicago indicated that fewer than 16% of students with similar credit deficiencies would graduate from high school with their peers (Miller, Allensworth, & Kochanek, 2002), so participants in my studies were at significant risk of dropping out of school.

In both studies, I recruited students through the schools' principals, asking them to connect me with students who fit the study's inclusion criteria. For my pilot study, I was looking for students who had been continuously enrolled in the school since entering as freshmen in fall 2005 and who had not earned enough credits to be promoted to 10th grade by spring 2007. The student participants were a convenience sample: those who agreed to participate and returned signed parental consent forms, on a first-come basis until I had three students at each school. In spring of their second year, students would have needed between 8 and 12 credits to be "on track" to graduate. Most students I spoke with still had fewer than 5 credits when I interviewed them. Study 1 included two young men and one young woman at Maxwell High School, and three young women at Devon High School. All the Maxwell High students were African American. At Devon I spoke with one African American, one Latina, and one White student.

For Study 2, I used the same basic criteria to select student participants in the next year's cohort: students who entered high school in fall 2006 and were still considered freshmen in spring 2008. I limited participants to African American females in both Devon and Alexander High Schools, as almost all students at Alexander were African American and all students at Devon were female. I recruited all available students who fit my inclusion criteria. Those who returned parental consent forms were included in the study. Table 4.2 lists the 14 students across Studies 1 and 2 and shows which school they attended, as well as basic demographic information for each student.

At the time of my student interviews, the peer group with whom students had entered high school 2 years earlier was finishing its sophomore year, nearly halfway to graduation. While their friends looked forward to 11th grade, my 14 participants had uncertain educational futures. Statistically, their odds of graduating from high school with their class were already less than one in five. Though they did not necessarily know it at the time, all of them would fail additional courses during the spring semester that our interviews took place.

It was striking to me how similar their 14 stories were as students described the experience of failing freshman courses and their attempts to recover credits. Regardless of which of the three schools they attended, their initial descriptions of failure were fairly indistinguishable. Chapter 5 tells these stories and identifies common themes across them. Students at all three schools described teacher problems, attendance problems, and teenager problems that led to poor grades. They talked in very similar terms about how failure felt and their recognition of the need to change. Chapter 6 looks at the effects of the schools' different grading policies on student failure and students' attempts to pull themselves out of failure. Chapter 7 focuses on students' experiences with credit recovery across the different schools. In short, while the initial causes and experiences of failure were similar for all 14 students, the paths of students in the two traditional schools were significantly complicated by an antiquated grading and credit system that functioned as intended. Once students started to fail, it seemed the system tried to weed them out, sometimes through the actions of well-meaning teachers and sometimes independently of them. In contrast, most students at Devon found ample support and opportunity to rectify the precarious situation in which their academic failure had put them.

Table 4.2. The Fourteen Students (all names are pseudonyms)

STUDY 1	
Maxwell High School	**Devon High School**
Dawson (*African American male*)	Courtney (*African American female*)
Rodney (*African American male*)	Juana (*Latina female*)
Sonia (*African American female*)	Tiffany (*White female*)
STUDY 2 (all African American females)	
Alexander High School	**Devon High School**
Kendra Monique Shana	Alisha Brittany Diamond
	Latrice Sharday

FIVE

10,000 Ways That Won't Work

The Frustration of Academic Failure

Thomas Alva Edison famously said, "I have not failed. I've just found 10,000 ways that won't work." This seems like a healthy attitude to have toward failure: Keep your eyes on the prize, learn from each attempt, and bounce back every time you fall short of success. But it would be hard for teenagers to adopt that approach in school because nobody around them is characterizing their academic failure in quite that light. Students make sense of failure in a social context, through social interaction, according to interpretive frameworks they share with significant adults, peers, family, and society at large. Students' experiences and interpretations of academic failure, in this sense, are constrained by the range of "plausible" interpretations available around them. And for the most part, school failure is seen as a pretty bad and shameful thing.

It is also hard to keep one's eyes on the prize when it is unclear exactly what the prize is. Most students are striving for a high school diploma, which seems very distantly related to tonight's algebra homework or the questions from Chapter 3 of *The Scarlet Letter*. Students seldom see the prize as specific kinds of knowledge and skills they would develop through schoolwork, in part because teachers seldom make that explicit. If my goal is to learn how to solve quadratic equations, then failing to solve some of them can give me useful information about what to do differently. But learning from failure only works if I know what I'm trying to learn, have a reason to learn it, get quality feedback on my efforts, and get to try again.

Unfortunately, as the students in my studies tried to pull themselves out of failure and get back on track to graduation, they hit one obstacle after another. In their first 18 months of high school, they found 10,000 ways that didn't work in their quest to develop knowledge and skills, pass classes, and earn credits.

Every student I spoke with entered high school expecting to be successful. Some felt a little trepidation at first—Dawson said, "I thought it was going to be scary, like how they show in the movies"—but most soon grew accustomed to their new school. The first time they failed a class, the students felt shocked, disappointed, discouraged; they had entered high school with high hopes, and failure took the wind out of their sails. Many of them stumbled around a bit afterward, but eventually they all gathered themselves up and resolved to do better. Unfortunately, failure seemed to breed failure: All 14 students failed additional classes even as they planned to recover credits from their earlier failures.

WHY STUDENTS FAILED

I asked students in all three schools to explain what happened in each failed course from their first year and a half of school. As I listened to their explanations, I was struck by a few thoughts. First, life can pose significant problems that undermined these kids at every turn. Lack of transportation, health problems, work responsibilities, housing instability, family trauma, and various outside obligations all interfered with students' schoolwork and contributed to their course failures. Students also ran into difficulties related to urban schools themselves: high teacher turnover, lack of resources, course scheduling, and just plain inadequate preparation from earlier schooling plagued students and significantly interfered with their academic success. For example, Brittany told me she hadn't had a teacher for most of 8th grade—literally did not have a teacher in the room for most of the year—because the principal could not find one willing to work in her elementary school. Brittany's poor performance as she entered 9th grade was hardly surprising.

It also became obvious, as students compared courses they failed with courses they were passing, that students weren't universally "bad" at school. A teenager might demonstrate very different behavior in English than in math, for example, either because of his natural interest in one subject over another or because something about the teacher particularly inspired or agitated him.

Lastly, 9th-graders are just big kids. They make poor choices. They often don't know how to manage interpersonal conflicts, particularly with adults who have power over them. They don't foresee logical consequences of their present actions. And for the most part they seem really disorganized. Many students made mistakes or miscalculations in the transition to high school that did not become apparent to them until it was too late. Some didn't like the school they had to attend and resisted being there, exercising their displeasure by refusing to engage in required work. Many talked about feeling incredibly bored and unable to force themselves to focus. Even with all this, students' shortcomings in maturity were often trumped or at least exacerbated by problems in the urban schools they attended or in their lives outside of school. Most important, nobody seemed to be cutting them any slack.

Problems with Teachers

Sharday attributed her failure in 9th-grade algebra to having a string of different teachers. She explained, "I had Mr. W at first. But then he left. Then we started with Ms. S. Then she [was] our teacher. When we get used to her, then we got Ms. D, and she was a brand-new teacher. She don't even know what you doing. She brand new. You got to teach her what you doing, and half the time you don't even know what you doing." Sharday painted a picture of adult disorganization and instruction so incoherent that I was kind of amazed anybody passed her math course.

Sometimes teachers were consistently there, but not helpful. Rodney failed two semesters of photography back to back because "I didn't have a camera, so that was our grade basically, we had to have a camera. My camera had got broken, like toward the middle of the school year, and I wasn't able to get another one." The teacher knew his situation, but offered no help. Given that he couldn't do any of the work, I asked Rodney if he stopped going to his photography class. "No," he told me. "I went to class every day."

All three Alexander students blamed the same English teacher for their having failed freshman literature. Shana told me, "I was doing my work every day. I just didn't understand how I fail. . . . But I was just looking around . . . like a lot of kids failed this class, the majority of students. [The school administrators] was wondering why all these kids had to go to summer school. So they fired [the teacher]." Kendra told me a similar story: "He didn't know how to teach, and he ended up getting fired because they used to observe him. Everybody, I mean almost the whole class, almost everybody failed." I asked her for specifics on his shortcomings as a teacher. "He made the class boring. He didn't give good examples. He don't know how to explain how to do the work. We'd end up half doing it and not doing it at all." Though the teacher apparently got fired, Alexander students all paid the price as they entered 10th grade without a required English credit.

Often, problems leading to course failure were not so egregious, boiling down to interpersonal conflicts between students and teachers. Students had little patience for teachers whom they perceived as inflexible or unsupportive. Latrice said she failed 10th-grade math because "my teacher's too petty. . . . She like to do lesson on lesson over lesson over lesson and we never do get a chance to go back and make things up [that we missed]. I don't like her." Monique's explanation for failing PE was succinct: "I wasn't dressing for gym 'cause that man would get on my nerve and he was a pervert. So I got a F in gym." Brittany told me her science teacher "just be playing, she be thinking this was a joke" when Brittany came after school for help. "She still just standing like I wasn't there, like I can keep coming up there for her. So I just don't even go to her" for help anymore. Sonia said her French teacher was "crazy. She's like a favoritism type of teacher. . . . She just acted different towards me, like a attitude type of way. So I stopped coming" to French class. Of course, skipping class was not the mature response, but unfortunately many students didn't have any better strategies for handling conflicts with teachers.

Problems with Attendance

Absences were a major contributor to student failure, primarily because they resulted in students not turning in work that was assigned when they weren't there. Sometimes students missed several days in a row, but even short-term absences seemed to take a large toll on students' course performance. Diamond said she failed humanities "because I missed this big project" when she went out of town "'cause my grandma had died." Latrice was failing language arts "probably 'cause I didn't come like the beginning of the school year. . . . I didn't know what [a missing assignment] was, so I just didn't do it."

Alisha had significant attendance problems, missing "like 40-something days" in freshman year. A paperwork glitch interfered with verifying her graduation from 8th grade, and "that made me miss like a month out of school" at the beginning of the year. Twice she missed school to attend funerals. Alisha also suffered from severe asthma, which often kept her home. Compounding the negative effects of her absences, Alisha thought teachers didn't want to be bothered with helping her catch up. When she returned to class after being gone, "most [teachers] they just don't ask nothing. They don't ask. They just . . . look. You know what I'm saying. . . . Some of them probably care. Some of them probably don't."

Regardless of the cause, absences contributed to students' further withdrawal from school. Monique had been the victim of an assault which, by her account, contributed to failing grades "'cause the beginning of my sophomore year, I had to keep running to court so I wasn't here." I asked whether teachers said anything to her when she missed school. "No," she told me. "None of them." As Monique continued to struggle and fail in school, she said her attitude worsened and she often didn't want to be there. "I come to school, but certain classes I'll be late for. I do that on purpose 'cause some teachers be boring me."

Dawson also missed classes selectively. His biology class "started out . . . I was doing good and all, but I got one of my hypotheses wrong on one of the little experiments, so [the teacher] gave me an F. I didn't think that was right. He could have gave me at least half credit for trying, but he gave me an F. . . . After that I just gave up and stopped going."

Sometimes students' problems were around scheduling. All three Maxwell students failed either first- or ninth-period because of its timing. To alleviate overcrowding, Maxwell programmed some students from first to eighth periods and others from second to ninth periods. Unfortunately, students didn't always get the shift they wanted. Rodney said he got an F in first-period algebra, which started at 7:45 A.M., because "I was taking the bus, and I couldn't make it there on time, 'cause I live so far away. It was hard for me to get up on time and make it out the house by a certain time to catch the bus at a certain time."

Dawson had the opposite problem: "I always come to school, just sometime I don't go to [my last] class. . . . They start me at 8:35, but every day I be here around 7:25. . . . I'd rather start first period than to start second." Because he often skipped his ninth-period class, he was "right now . . . on the verge of failing." Sonia tried to switch to an earlier schedule so she could get a ride home with her sister. Instead she stopped going to ninth-period biology because "I didn't wanna walk home."

Suspensions added to student absences. Kendra repeatedly got suspended in sophomore year, which she said made it very difficult to get any traction in her efforts to catch up academically. Whenever she returned from a 5-day suspension, "It's hard 'cause . . . I gotta still do my classwork, but then I gotta catch up on 5 days of work in every class. And we got seven classes, so I gotta do like 5 days of seven classes' classwork and homework, and then I gotta stay on with the regular work and homework. It's too much." The first time she was suspended, Kendra contacted teachers in advance to get work to complete during her absence, but only two teachers gave her assignments. "And nobody else, they act like they don't care. Don't nobody else give me no work. So I don't come up here no more to ask for work. I just get suspended."

The behavior of some teachers made Kendra feel increasingly disheartened about her chances of succeeding in school: "If they see the situation that I'm in, I'm getting bad grades, I ain't doing so well. If they care, they won't suspend me over little things, because they won't want me to fall behind. Unless it's something major like a fight or something like that. But they suspend me for stupid stuff." Kendra said she was suspended for things like "spitting" water when she started laughing while using a drinking fountain or "poking" a boy's hand with a comb during class. She said her behavior was the same in every classroom, but that some teachers repeatedly suspended her while others never did.

Problems with Being a Teenager

Students attributed many failures to their own lack of organizational skills, self-motivation strategies, or general maturity. As Dawson said about his algebra course, "It was my goofy ways that kept me from passing the class." Monique failed geometry because "I put my book in my friend's locker and she lost it. Like 3 months ago. It affects my grade a lot 'cause when I had my book I was doing good. . . . Geometry ain't that hard." Sonia failed most of her freshman classes because her social life became more interesting than her classwork. She said, "First semester, at the beginning, you know, I was on my stuff. 'Cause my dad told me you gotta go to high school, you gotta wanna go to college, and all this other stuff, so I was on it. But then I get in there and I see all my friends from elementary school and I'm like, talking and stuff and, yep, everything went down the drain." In reflection, Sonia said, "I guess it might be every person that's around that age 13, 14, and they start to change and think that school don't matter no more, or whatever . . . like, I'm too grown for all this stuff."

Diamond failed most of her 9th-grade courses because of poor organizational skills. "I was so unorganized that stuff was just everywhere. I turned in stuff late, some was early, because I wasn't organized." Juana had similar difficulties: "The problem with me is I wasn't turning in my work." She found it challenging to manage multiple classes. "I had . . . a whole bunch of homework in this class, and homework in this class, and I kinda did homework in other classes and not this class." In humanities, "my journals were all over the place, like I would just flip to a random page, write everything down, next class flip to another random page, write everything down, so my work was just everywhere."

Brittany avoided work altogether. "If they gave us homework I wouldn't do it at all. I wouldn't even mention homework to my mother. I didn't write it down so when I go home, I come back to school with no homework." Even when she completed homework, "sometime when I do it I don't turn it in. I don't know why." Brittany also had difficulty staying on task. "I focus on doing other stuff than my work. . . . I'm in class talking and by the time I start my work the bell ring and it's time to go."

Some students got in trouble early in 9th grade by miscalculating the importance of staying on top of schoolwork. At Devon High, where teachers gave *Not Yets* instead of Fs, students thought getting an NY was no big deal. As Tiffany explained:

> Most girls here, they take advantage of the *Not Yet* system, 'cause they think they can just go ahead keep getting NYs and NYs and there nothing going to happen. And you know, they can't do that . . . 'cause once you get one NY you're going to think that it's okay and you gonna get some more, some more, some more and they just pile up. 'Cause that's how it used to be [for me]. It used to start piling up.

Dawson thought many of his peers at Maxwell did poorly in the beginning of 9th grade because some kids "made it seem like it wasn't a big deal, so everybody is thinking like it's cool to just play around." He said that on the first-quarter report card, "them grades don't count. . . . I think it's like every second report card count as a credit, so this report card we're about to get [for third quarter], it don't count. It's just a grade, but the report card in June count as a credit." Although Dawson was technically correct that only semester grades were recorded on students' transcripts and used to determine whether students earned credits, students' quarter grades were almost always averaged into the final semester grade. Students like Dawson who failed the first quarter usually found themselves unable to pass the semester.

Sonia talked about the stark differences between 8th and 9th grades. "Elementary school you got to stand in a single file line, you got to wait for the teacher to take you [anywhere]. And basically high school is just . . . if you want independence, like I said, there's nobody standing over your back trying to make sure you do everything like you supposed to." Sonia "messed up" her freshman year because she "took advantage of that all the way. Nobody watching me, nobody really care." She said it made her just kind of run wild.

Sharday described her academic performance as "up and down, up and down" as she ineffectively turned her attention from one subject to another: "So then I had to put time on this one, but then be taking time from off this one." Though each student at Alexander was given a planner at the start of the year to keep track of school assignments, Sharday confessed she "just wasn't using" it. She shrugged her shoulders and added with a wry smile, "I'm a teenager."

GETTING WHAT THEY DESERVE

Ninth-graders failed courses because things inside and outside school interfered with their academic work—often resulting in extensive absences—and because they were typical teenagers with "goofy ways." As teenagers, they didn't plan well. They acted very irrationally. They lost a book and didn't do anything about it. They got a bad attitude and acted out when they perceived a teacher was not helping them. Clearly, these behaviors were counterproductive. Part of the goal of high school is to help students develop other, more effective ways of handling such challenges. But none of this should be unexpected: These were shockingly predictable 14-year-old responses.

Melissa Roderick at the University of Chicago tells the story of a CPS high school principal who was deeply affected by a study from the Consortium on Chicago School Research showing that even a few additional days of absence in a semester reduced a student's chance of graduating from high school by a significant percentage.[1] The principal taped the graphic showing this relationship to the side of her computer. Every time a student was sent to her office for misbehavior, the principal asked herself if the student's offense was worth cutting in half his chance of graduating on time. She issued significantly fewer suspensions using that rule of thumb.

I would pose the same question here. Certainly, many of the behaviors students described that led to their failures were immature and ill-advised. But were their transgressions so egregious that they deserve to earn $260,000 less in their lifetimes, to greatly increase their chances of incarceration, to die sooner? I am not being hyperbolic; this is the basic calculus now governing their lives. Failing 9th-grade classes *greatly* increases students' chances of dropping out of high school—and lower wages, higher likelihood of going to jail, and earlier deaths are among the average consequences of dropping out. In Chicago, as in other urban districts, upwards of 40% of students drop out of school rather than graduate. We can very accurately identify future dropouts by their failure of two or more 9th-grade classes. That was how I identified the kids in my studies. *These are the students who drive the dropout statistics*, and often they fail courses for dumb reasons.

Using Feather's (1999) framework on deservingness (from Chapter 2), we might think students deserve to suffer bad consequences when their failure is the result of their own bad behavior. I'm all in favor of bad consequences for bad behavior. I would just like to see consequences in line with the severity of students' offenses. The long-term consequences of course failure are likely to be severe and completely disproportional to the poor choices students described here. When my own kids were little, I wanted them to learn to play nicely with other children. If they hit someone with a stick in the park, I may have intervened and taken away the stick, but I would not have broken their fingers. I wanted them to learn a lesson, but without inflicting permanent harm in the process. Failing 14-year-olds for immature academic behavior seems to me the equivalent of breaking the fingers of preschoolers for overly aggressive play—in both cases the problematic behaviors are *what one should expect* given young people's developmental phase. Our role as adults should be to help kids learn better behaviors without causing them irreparable harm.

Ninth-graders need to learn to organize their work, plan their time, and take care of their school responsibilities before doing more fun things that they might rather do. Unfortunately, failing students does not help develop any of those skills. Teenagers also need to understand the importance of attending every class, every day. When teachers ignore students returning from an absence, it reinforces the idea that it doesn't matter if students are there or not. From the students' perspective, no one seems to have noticed they were missing. Repeatedly suspending students for minor infractions may send a very similar message about the importance of being in the classroom. Students who fail classes should get what they deserve. But I think what they deserve may well be a group of adults who will both hold them accountable without vilifying them and teach them how to rise to the challenges of high school.

HOW IT FEELS TO FAIL

Alisha was telling me how hard her humanities class was. Every week she got a long list of vocabulary words she had trouble remembering, and she kept failing her tests. I asked her some of the words she had learned. "I can't remember," she told me. "It's a lot of them." I kidded with her: Couldn't she remember at least one? "Uh . . . yeah," she said quietly. "*Inadequate.*" I repeated it back: "*Inadequate.* Okay. And what's that mean?" Alisha lowered her head. "Uh, it mean . . . *not enough.*"

Bringing home a report card with failing grades elicited a range of emotions, from inadequacy to anger to embarrassment to frustration. For most students in my studies, getting Fs was a new experience. "I was shocked when I first knew that I was failing," Dawson told me, "because I ain't never failed before."

Diamond was also surprised by her failing grades: "I was, like, wow. I don't know how to feel. It was kind of confused, kind of sad, kind of mad, it was mixed feelings. I did a lot of work, I really tried hard, and then, it was like, dang! I'm failing all my classes." Diamond's initial reaction was typical of many of her peers: to give up. "At first I was like, I'm not doing it anymore 'cause I'm not about to keep trying and I keep failing." This sentiment lasted a few months and Diamond's grades continued to fall, adding to her frustration: "Every time I did something, it seemed like I fall back down. Ugh. I'm *done* trying." Diamond said the thing that made school difficult was the work itself; she had no strategies for how to do it. "If I don't understand something, I'm just going to give up and be like, I'm not doing it." By the end of the year, she was too far behind to pass most of her classes and it looked like she would have to repeat 9th grade. The thought of having to go to summer school "was embarrassing, and it made me sad. I cried. I didn't want to be the only one, like if my friends leave me, and I was going to be the only one still stuck."

Latrice was "mad, but I didn't show it," when she got her first bad report card. As her grades continued to fall, she got "frustrated" and considered quitting altogether. "I didn't want to come to school. I just didn't feel like it." She was embarrassed about not being promoted to 10th grade. "Everybody knows then I was on a borderline failing, and I was not fixing to fail."

Courtney was also surprised by her first failing report card. "I expected a lot more, just for the fact that I knew the material." In retrospect, she realized that "I just didn't show it out to the teacher, so they don't really know that I know it. . . . You actually have to do the work to get what you know shown."

Monique's response to failing was defiance: "It makes you kind of really want to rebel against them or something." The hardest thing about trying to improve her grades, she said, was that "I can't stay focused on one thing long. I be doing my work, but then I get tired of doing it. So I just push it aside so then it'd be incomplete. I go do something else."

Sharday had been a good student in elementary school, and failing classes in high school did not sit well with her. "It kind of felt bad. 'Cause you always had like somebody on your shoulder telling you, 'You need [it], you gotta get it.' So you feel like you got this person on your shoulder wanting you to do this all the time, but you can't." The worst part was the public nature of her failure. "I knew that if I didn't pass summer school, I was gonna have this class again. And you don't want the same class again, knowing all the rest of the kids pass."

For Shana, getting failing grades made her really question who she was and what she was doing. "You feel like you are just—you're not good. You just wonder why you're in the predicament that you in right now." She was particularly aware of how failing affected her family. "I have little sisters that's under me, and they look up to me. I just want to show them that I'm better, you know? Make sure, if they look up to me, I'm a good role model to them, that I make sure I can guide them so they don't look at the bad things, you know?" Shana took full responsibility for her "predicament." "I blame everything on myself. I don't blame it on nobody else. I just blame it on myself 'cause I know I should have worked harder."

The students I spoke with at Devon, Maxwell, and Alexander High Schools shared a range of emotions about failure. Thus far in our conversations, it would have been hard to sort out which student went to which school. Many said that at some point it felt hopeless to keep trying. They talked about wanting to give up, to transfer to another school, even to drop out. They were mad, discouraged, embarrassed, frustrated, ashamed, defiant. Regardless of the school they attended, students' feelings about course failure were quite similar.

THE NEED TO CHANGE

Though students' initial reaction to failing grades was to feel deflated and to want to give up, eventually each of them resolved to work harder and turn things around. This usually happened when they realized the consequences of continuing down their present path. Oyserman and James (2009) referred to an awareness of the "gap . . . between one's current level of effort and the effort required" to accomplish one's desired goal (p. 2). Students described coming to awareness of this gap and vowed to work harder and get better grades. They often framed this as "growing up" or reaching a new level of maturity.

Alisha realized she would not be promoted to 10th grade if she did not start completing her schoolwork. "I gotta make up this work, and then if I don't make it up, they probably drop me [back to 9th grade and] I'm gonna have to repeat." Diamond seemed to have given up in the middle of freshman year, but then in the spring, "they was like, if you don't do this you don't pass. I'm like, I don't pass? Well, I gotta do this 'cause I want to pass." Her grades suffered from lost and misplaced work and missing her morning classes. She told me she "want[ed] to do something different" like "I would make sure I was organized, and I would get to school on time." Diamond said her realization was not sudden; it "was like a growth thing. It was like it grew into me then made me realize that I just had to do something besides just come to school to look at the board." Reflecting on her behavior in 9th grade, she said, "Why would I just sit in the classroom and do nothing? That's crazy. I realized that I have to come to school and do some work, actually do work."

Juana decided there was no alternative to turning things around. "Last year when I was like the lowest of the low, I felt depressed. I didn't want to go to school. But there was something in me that said I had to go to school, so I went." Sonia failed almost all her classes in the first semester of high school, and then most second-semester classes as well. She explained, "Everybody try to change when, well, it's not too late, but, like at the end. I tried to change at the end." She didn't put concerted effort into turning herself around until the following year. That fall, "I'm thinking like . . . I want to graduate with everybody in my class, 2009, so get on the ball, do my work now. I think I'm doing much better this year. At the beginning of the year I was slacking again, but I have to look like, you know, it's time to start."

Dawson also waited until his 2nd year of high school before making changes. "I found myself looking back at the same thing [this year], but now I changed it. So I decided I'm going to stay in 9th [grade], stop cutting and stuff, and keep on going. 'Cause I ain't trying to be stuck. . . . I want to go to the next grade."

Courtney admitted her epiphanies were frequent but short-lived when she got bad grades. "Every time I get my report card or my progress report, I change for about a week, do all my homework, but then I just start getting lazy again and it just stops." I asked her why she even tries to change. "Because I know I can do better," she told me.

Some students' freshman failures had less to do with academics and more to do with social aspects of high school. Here, too, students vowed to make changes. Latrice attributed much of her trouble in 9th grade to conflicts with classmates. Although she liked many students, some of them "is just straight out ridiculous. They whole career is based on talking about somebody. . . . Last year I was fed into it 'cause I'm the type of person, when you say something to me, I'm gonna say something back." At some point, however, when Latrice saw how her behavior was affecting her academic standing, "I had to realize that that wasn't getting me nowhere. And it sure wasn't getting them nowhere 'cause they was gonna continue to do it even if I said something. So I decided, stop saying stuff to people."

Sharday had a similar realization in 10th grade about her defiant behavior. After rebelling against her grandmother for sending her to Devon against her wishes, Sharday made friends with a student who actually "liked the school." She found that "my mind starting to change. I'm like, ain't no use to be acting like this. You stuck here. You might as well like it." Echoing Diamond's earlier sentiments, Sharday could "start feeling myself growing. You know, people grow. They change they thoughts. Everything change."

The question is, once students change their thoughts, is that all it takes? Dawson felt like he knew how to turn things around in his schoolwork: "Limit my playing [and] talking. Pay more attention in class. Work harder. 'Cause usually if I didn't get it, I just give up on it." But if he didn't get it, could sheer force of will change his performance? With new resolve, each of the 14 students tried to do better, generally by "working harder." Unfortunately, they ran into problems.

First, though they aspired to do well, some were ambivalent about being a "good student." Perhaps this conflicted with what they saw as their "true self" or with the image they held of themselves within their peer group, but for whatever reason, the image of the good student was not one they could all fully embrace. Second, no one really seemed to know *how to become* a good student. They tried to force themselves to work harder and focus, but often they found schoolwork exceedingly boring and could not maintain the required degree of effort. They had no strategies to improve their performance. Third, in the case of students at the two traditional high schools, structural barriers got in their way. It turns out it was not always possible to turn things around in a class.

Being a Good Student

On one hand, Monique said, "I expect me to pick my grades up 'cause they ain't looking that hot right now. . . . [I expect to] do well in my classes, go to college." On the other hand, Monique was ambivalent about changing her behavior. After describing her image of a "good student," I asked

Monique if she honestly wished she were more like that. "Yeah, I would like to be a good student. But I don't want to be no, you know, person that always thinking about nothing but books, books, books, books, books. [But] I wouldn't mind being on the honor roll. It would be nice."

Dawson pointed out the tension between doing well in school and feeling connected to peers. "The main thing about high school," he told me, "like you see on the movies and stuff, is about popularity. . . . Some people, they'll do stupid stuff just to be cool." He said sometimes you have friends that support you in being a good student, "then in other cases you feel like you want to push yourself so much that you gonna have to let the person that you like the most, you gonna have to let 'em go, so you can be able to do what you gotta do. You could go back to them later on." He paused for a minute. "That is one of the hardest things. Let go one of your closest friends, to get through with school."

Sonia struggled between her social persona and being a good student. In her world, "the populars" were clearly a different crowd from the students who were doing well in school. She had a hard time seeing how a person could be simultaneously popular and "smart," but it was clear she wanted to have what each of these personas would get her: social belonging and academic success. "Smart kids, they might get talked about, but . . . the others they might be the populars, and they can breeze through [the social aspects], but they still struggling in school. And the smart people get talked about but . . . they passing, they own it."

Shana also expressed the tension she felt between doing what was academically advantageous and being socially accepted: "A good student is like, a person who comes on time. A teacher pet. Basically, to me that just a teacher pet. And a teacher pet is a person who just do all the work, you know, getting they grades up, staying after school, in a lot of programs. They have good behavior. They respect each other." I asked how other kids in the class felt about good students. "I think they look at them differently. Like, they just want so much attention, they a teacher pet. . . . But I don't say that to [them]. Like, some of my friends, they real good. I don't say that to them. I congratulate them for what they doing. They like a role model to me. I just look at them, like, yeah, I should do like her and what she doing." Shana then proceeded to tell me how she was not a good student: "Coming in late. Missing some of the work." Being a good student, "it just, it's too much."

Rodney felt enormous pressure to do well in school. Although he gave himself a "90% chance" of graduating on time with his classmates, he also acknowledged significant barriers to reaching that goal:

> Like problems outside of school. Trying to feel comfortable in school. . . . I feel like it's a burden on my shoulder. The only person that graduated in my family is my brother. . . . He's 25 now. . . . My oldest brother

didn't graduate; he dropped out [at] 16. . . . My mother didn't graduate.
. . . I feel like everybody pressuring me, like, "You gotta graduate, you gotta graduate." I understand that I gotta do it, but I don't like people just trying to push me.

Although Rodney sometimes believed he could succeed, he also had serious doubts. The pressure from family members seemed to exacerbate his uncertainty.

For some adolescents, the image of a good student just felt unobtainable. Kendra described people who "get good grades. They on honor roll. They stay consistent with their work. They're not disruptive in class. They don't get suspended." I asked Kendra in what ways was she like a good student. "I don't know," she said quietly. "I got potential, but I just . . . I don't know."

"I Gotta Just Strive"

American culture portrays academic success as an entirely individual enterprise, and the 14 students in my studies had come to internalize the idea that doing better in school meant pulling themselves up by their bootstraps. I heard this as Dawson described his struggles in math class: "Like geometry, I don't know how I'm going to pull it off. I got a clue like, I gotta just strive, work harder for what I need. [I'll get it] if I really want it and believe I can pass it." I asked Dawson if he felt it was totally dependent on *him* to improve. "Yeah, it's on me. It's not on the teacher. I can't rely on the teacher all the time to help me. I gotta try to work it out for myself sometimes." Rodney expressed similar sentiments. When I asked what was going to make the difference between him graduating or not, he replied, "Me. Me, myself." He said there was nothing the school could or would do to help him.

These students all seemed to interpret their failure as being entirely their own responsibility. This is not surprising, as the notion of individual achievement is consistently reinforced by traditional high school structures, policies, and practices signaling to students that they are on their own in overcoming barriers to learning. In interviews with British youth who dropped out of school, Smyth and Hattam (2001) reported that some young people engaged in "needlessly blaming themselves [for their failure] . . . rather than overtly criticising schooling and school processes" (p. 410). Meyer, Scott, and Deal (1983) made a similar observation: "Even students who are academic failures and frequently truant tend to define their schools as very satisfactory. The schools succeed in maintaining support even among those whom they process into failure" (pp. 56–57).

I asked each student why some people succeeded in high school while others dropped out. Sonia put responsibility solely on the individual student:

"The ones that make it, they want something, they want something in life. The ones that just give up, gave up on life. That's how I see it. They just gave up." I asked who or what was responsible for the ones who gave up. "It's their responsibility," she replied. "One hundred percent."

Juana expressed a similar sentiment about students who drop out of school. "I put it on them, because they can't blame other people for how they're doing. It's all on them." Courtney felt like students' outcomes were fated from the beginning:

> The ones that just breeze through, they obviously have a goal that they need to achieve and it's their own personal goal. That's how they grew up, 'cause you can't just change how you are right away. Like, if you are always one to do homework, you're always going to do homework. And if you struggle, you're always going to struggle. And if you don't like school to begin with, you're going to drop out of school eventually.

Even when adults intervened to help, they tended to frame failing students' situations as individual struggles that students had to step up to face. After Sonia failed most of her freshman classes, she said the school

> had me talk to someone, I think she's a case worker. And she was just telling me, "At the end, you've got to want all of this for yourself, because all these people that go here now is not going to matter when you get older. When you decide to have kids, you want to provide for them, and provide for your family, and you know, you got to want it for yourself at the end, 'cause all that's going to matter is you." So, I was just like, I gotta do this.

It was striking to me that when I asked Sonia a little later in our conversation if there were any adults in school she could go to for help, perhaps this case worker, she shrugged and said, "Yeah, but, like I said, it don't seem like nobody care. That's what I'm saying, in the end, all that matters is you. You gotta want it for yourself. That's why I'm trying to pull myself up."

In the abstract, Sonia held every student responsible for her own fate. But she gave a different response when I asked specifically about how she would design a school for students like herself. What would her ideal school do to help students be successful? She thought for a long time, and then said very quietly:

> A lot more help and . . . a lot more attention for some kids. Some kids that's in my predicament, they gotta cry for attention. And like, they want to be heard, but some of 'em feel like they messed up this one time, nobody want to hear what they got to say. Don't nobody want to be

bothered, don't nobody care . . . [so] overall, more attention and more
school time. Just . . . a little push.

Needing a Strategy

Like virtually every student, Rodney's strategy for improving his grades
was to "work harder." He went on to say it was a matter of getting "a better
understanding of things. Like the whole thing with my grades, it's not that
I don't know how to do it, it's like, I just need an explanation, or a better
understanding of it. If I understand something, it's easy . . . it'll stick to my
mind. But if I don't understand it, it's like, I don't know how to do it, and
it'll frustrate me. And that's when I just throw it to the side." When I asked
him his strategy for dealing with this, he went back to "working hard." "As
I say, I'm gonna work harder, like, I try everything to get a better, clearer
view of it. And once I get that clear view, there's nothing holding me back
from doing the work." Similarly, Dawson said he was very motivated to
"start going to class more, start working harder, 'cause I know I can do the
work." But when he bumped up against academic challenge, "It's just, if the
work is hard I just stop. I just give up on it."

Sonia also had a mental list of what to do to pass classes: "Paying attention, taking my notes . . . listening to the teacher, blocking everything else
out." I asked if she knew how to do that. Was she pretty good at taking notes,
listening, doing the whole "student thing"? "No!" she laughed. "But I try
my hardest, though." Later, she became more reflective. Since coming to high
school, she had struggled with math, chemistry, and biology. She wanted to
learn those subjects. "You have to learn it to get to college. That's what it is.
I mean, I wouldn't mind doing geometry. . . . When I was in grammar school,
I used to love math when the right person come to me and teach it to me and
break it down and show me and stuff." Now the work seemed to have gotten
a lot harder. I asked Sonia about students who did well in those classes. Did
they know how to do something that she was not sure how to do? "Um, I
don't know. . . . I used to think they was just smart, but . . . most people that
I talk to now, they like, 'Well, I just listen, I just pay attention, I don't know
everything they doing so I get help' or whatever. And I'm like, well, that's the
same thing I been trying to do, but it don't seem to work for me."

What I found heartbreaking as I listened to these students was how
isolated they were from the kinds of real strategies that would help them
approach the academic challenges they faced. The research evidence across
a wide number of studies shows that having access to concrete strategies for
tackling academic tasks is highly predictive of students' success in school.

Effective academic strategies are tools students can use to improve their
school performance—things like setting goals for each piece of work they do,

dividing tasks into manageable chunks, monitoring their comprehension as they read, identifying what an assignment is asking them to do and picking the right approach to doing that, having a toolkit of approaches to choose from, manipulating information in different ways so they really start to understand it, distinguishing between the parts they understand and the parts that are confusing, asking for help when they need it, and having ways to refocus when they get distracted. Students with appropriate learning strategies are much more likely to stick with difficult tasks and persevere when they encounter obstacles (Farrington et al., 2012). They are more likely to believe that "I can succeed" and that "my ability and competence can grow"—academic mindsets that support and sustain student effort. And obviously, students who know how to tackle assignments, who put in more effort and don't give up when things get hard, are much more likely to pass classes. Without effective learning strategies, it looks like students just aren't trying hard enough. So we admonish them to "work harder" and to "want it more."

"BORING AND LEARNING DON'T MIX"

One major obstacle to academic success was that students found so much of school so incredibly boring. In describing high school courses, students repeatedly talked about being unable to maintain focus in deadening classroom environments. As Diamond put it, "Boring and learning—that just don't mix." She said when classes were "boring, then you don't focus. You're not focusing no more."

From an adult perspective, it is easy to see this as a lame excuse. As a former high school English teacher, I vividly remember students complaining to me that the book we were reading was boring, grammar was boring, everything was boring. It seemed like any time they didn't want to do something, they complained that it was boring. I continually struggled to make things *not* boring. But as I have traded my place as the instructor in a classroom for a seat as an observer of many teachers in many high schools over many years, I have come to a greater appreciation for students' plight. As they move from class to class, day after day, week after week, very little actually happens. For most of each day, grown-ups talk at them, explaining things, giving instructions, chastising them. I would not wish a daily 7-consecutive-hours-in-a-desk upon any adult I know. I'm amazed that teenagers in high school are as compliant with this arrangement as they are.

The students I spoke with had a particularly difficult time staying interested when they did not know what the teacher was talking about, causing them to disengage further. Lack of attention and lack of understanding thus reinforced each other in a vicious downward spiral. Diamond said if she can't understand what the teacher is teaching, "I kind of wander off. I be in my own little world. Sometimes I go to sleep, sometimes I be having a conversation with somebody else who don't really get it." Shana described her experience in one class she was struggling to pass: "Most of the time you're just kind of sitting there, and he's talking. . . . And I just nod off and go to sleep."

Courtney said she fell asleep in class because "I don't like always being lectured. . . . I think that's really boring. Sometimes I don't even need to fall asleep, but just by having someone talking and talking and talking, I just get, you know, annoyed with it, and I just put my head down and I won't wake up until someone's poking me, 'Get up, it's time to go to our next class.'" I asked Monique about math, where she had her head on the desk in one class I observed. "It's boring when you don't have it. You don't know what they're talking about." Tiffany had difficulty engaging in science class. "I'm the type of person—I'm a kinesthetic learner, so I like to do stuff with my hands. . . . We just read a lot and it was boring. . . . I don't *want* to do that, it's boring."

Sharday lamented that "I don't even like coming to school 'cause it be boring. They do the same thing over and over. I just don't want to waste my time. Just send me home." She said she has to "keep at myself to [be] doing something" to stay focused in class. Other than a river trip with her science class, which she really loved, Brittany shook her head trying to think of another example of something interesting in school. Monique offered this advice to teachers: "Don't make it boring. You know, you boring. They be talking, talking, talking, talking, talking, talking. You know [students] gonna wind up falling asleep."

The good news was that not *everything* was boring. In interesting classes, students found it much easier to engage and worked harder to be successful. Rodney particularly liked Spanish class because he found it relevant to his interests: "I really wanted to learn a new language, so I tried really hard to learn Spanish. I was doing all my homework, studying extra on the side, going to the library getting Spanish books to read, like, try to understand." As a result, he got As in Spanish on every report card.

Courtney liked both art and Spanish. Compared to other classes where she was putting down her head and falling asleep, art and Spanish kept her attention. In Spanish, "We get up and . . . do like little skits or whatever about stuff. 'Cause we're learning about insects and about, like, the river and how to say the words. So we did this presentation today . . . putting all those words together saying, 'Don't eat me,' 'I'm going to run away' or whatever, stuff like that." Because the class was fun and active, she stayed engaged.

Sometimes what made a class interesting was a good teacher who conveyed the material clearly. In general, Sonia said she failed classes because it was hard to focus amid all the distractions, particularly other people in the room. I asked her, "When you're in class, say you're in American Lit, is most of what's on your mind American Lit, or is most of what's on your mind who's in class, and what else is going on with people?" She laughed. "Mmm, when I'm in American Lit, she a pretty good teacher, so I be thinking about American Lit. I mean, she know how to explain things, she know how to go through it, you know, to make sure every individual student know what they doing." As a result, Sonia was passing English while she was failing most of her other classes. When something is interesting, Diamond concluded, "I pay more attention to it." Kendra concurred: "When work be fun, I be more focused. But if it be real boring, my mind slip away."

APPLYING PSYCHOLOGICAL RESEARCH TO STUDENT EXPERIENCE

Researchers who study student motivation and learning have long known that people put forth effort to learn when they value a task, expect positive results, and have strategies that help them successfully engage in the work. Developmental psychologists tell us that adolescents at 14 and 15 years old are only just beginning to think abstractly, to anticipate consequences, and to develop executive functions—the ability to regulate their own thoughts, behaviors, and emotions. Teenagers' attention tends to be focused on the present and on their place in the social world, with little thought to future responsibilities. Adolescents also tend to be really inconsistent, demonstrating remarkable maturity one minute in one context, and acting totally irrationally the next minute in a different context. They really aren't the most reliable or focused creatures on the planet.

Students who talked to me about their experiences with failure all wanted to do well in school. But to an incredible extent, they seemed to be given wide latitude to mess up. They were largely left to their own devices to figure out how to be successful, and they had only vague ideas about how to bring about success in many of their classes. They knew they needed to work harder, but they didn't know how to make themselves do that, particularly if they didn't understand what was going on in the classroom or couldn't maintain interest in what they were supposed to be learning. As a result, they kept failing. Over the course of the 2 years I talked with students for these projects, I was repeatedly struck with the awareness that students' academic failure was not due to any fatal character flaws or mental deficiencies, but rather to very normal and easily anticipated adolescent behavior.

I also found it most interesting to hear the shifts in students' voices when they moved from talking about their failed classes to talking about the classes in which they were doing well. Their eyes tended to light up, their speech became more animated, and they suddenly sounded like responsible, dedicated students: putting in extra work, looking forward to class, talking excitedly about what they were learning. Students seemed to undergo an amazing transformation when a teacher sparked their interest.

Yet, for all 14 students, failure was an ongoing burden, a weight they struggled to get out from under. Students across the three schools described very similar reasons for failing classes and very similar feelings about the experience of failure. At some point, however, their stories started to diverge. The young women attending Devon High School started sounding more hopeful. While their peers at Maxwell and Alexander described a sense of isolation and mystification about how to pull themselves out of increasingly dire situations, the Devon students talked of support they were receiving to catch up in their classes. Chapter 6 describes the role of grading practices in student failure across the three schools and in students' attempts to pass classes once they fell behind. Chapter 7 charts students' experiences as they followed the avenues laid out by their respective schools for credit recovery once they had failed a class. My hypothesis was that the century-old sorting mechanisms built into the traditional high schools would kick in to weed students out, but how exactly might that play out?

SIX

Falling into an Abyss

The Role of Grading in Student Failure

In a 2006 article on poverty and school reform, David Berliner made an interesting observation about poverty in the United States. He noted first that the percentage of nonpoor Americans who *became* poor due to temporary circumstance was roughly equivalent to the percentages of people who became poor in several other industrialized countries. A comparison of the number of those people who *remained* in poverty 3 years later, however, showed that the U.S. rate was significantly higher than those of our international counterparts. Berliner argued that while people anywhere in the world could fall into situational poverty—reasons of job loss, divorce, illness, or childbirth were most often the causes in this country—the United States had relatively "few mechanisms to get people out of poverty once they fall into poverty" (p. 10). Once Americans became poor, they tended to stay poor.

I wondered about the parallel to schools and failure: Is the problem not that we have too much academic failure, but rather that we have too few mechanisms to help students out of failure once they fall into it? This might help to explain why, once students start to fail, they tend to continue failing, as though failure were a bottomless abyss. As described in Chapter 1, school achievement has four interrelated dimensions—structural, academic, developmental, and motivational—that reinforce each other such that success tends to breed success, and failure breeds further failure. The next three chapters will illustrate in detail how these processes played out for the young people in my studies. Chapters 6 and 7 focus on the grading and credit systems, along with remediation and credit recovery programs, in the three high schools—looking at mechanisms for getting kids out of failure once they fell into it. The present chapter begins with a description of the structural features of the schools' grading policies and then explores how well these different structures met the academic, developmental, and motivational needs of students.

Thus far, we've seen that our 14 students, regardless of where they went to school, had very similar reasons for failing classes and very similar feelings about failure. At some point, they all resolved to do better. They had internalized the notion that the road to academic redemption lay in "trying harder." Unfortunately, as time went on, they all continued to fail classes. This was true for students in all three schools. Differences in grading and credit systems across the three schools did not seem to have any impact on the initial occurrence of course failure. Ninth-graders were losing credits and falling *into* failure similarly across schools. But could a different grading and credit system change students' ability to rally back once they fell behind or change the rate at which students recovered credit after they failed a class? By creating an alternative approach to grading and credit, did Devon High School offer students a better mechanism to get *out* of failure once they fell into it?

GRADING PRACTICES IMPEDE RECOVERY FROM FAILURE

Differences in school grading systems had big implications for students' ability to catch up again if they fell behind. One of the academic mindsets presented in Chapter 3 is the belief that "my ability and competence grow with my effort." If grades are an indication of a student's ability and competence, the different school grading systems sent very different messages about the payoffs to student effort. Where Alexander and Maxwell students seemed resigned to passivity in a system outside of their control, students at Devon expressed a much stronger sense of ownership and a better understanding of the grades they received. Devon students were convinced that their ability and competence would grow—and their grades would improve commensurately—if they put in the work their teachers laid out for them.

Most of my conversations around classroom grading practices took place within the context of Study 2, so most of the interview data presented here come from Alexander and Devon High Schools. I include data from interviews with Maxwell students where relevant.

Points, Letters, Carrots, Sticks: Grading in Alexander High School

As stated previously, Alexander and Maxwell High Schools utilized a traditional point and letter grade system. Grading consisted of a combination of the following practices: giving points for work completed without assessing its accuracy; marking right and wrong answers on individual assignments, quizzes, or tests and adding up points for correct answers; using rubrics to evaluate assignments based on specified criteria; and giving extra credit for additional work or to reward specific behaviors. Each assignment, project, paper, or test was worth a certain number of points, and a student's grade on each piece of graded work was determined by the points earned as a percentage of the points possible: Students who earned 90% or more of the possible points got an A, 80–89% was a B, and so on. The same calculation was used to derive a final letter grade for the course. Students needed at least 60% of total possible points for the semester (a grade of D–) to pass the class and receive course credit. Students earned one half-credit for passing each semester course. Students who failed a class (with less than 60% of possible points) earned no credit and had to retake the entire semester course (or its equivalent) to recover that half-credit.

Each Alexander teacher I interviewed was very cognizant that grades had a certain kind of power. They all discussed ways they tried to use their point system to extrinsically motivate and reward students for engaging in aspects of the class the teacher most valued. Social studies teacher Mr. Larken (all teacher names in the book are pseudonyms) said he had three categories of work—tests and quizzes, homework, and classwork—each worth a certain percentage of a student's total grade. He also "threw in kind of random grades here and there for participation, attendance, and preparation" for up to 15% of the total grade. Mr. Larken emphasized the importance of students completing assignments, which he saw as fundamental to their learning and engagement in class. He weighted his grading system to reward this behavior. "Students that might never pass a test, they could still end up getting as high as a C in the class if they're doing their homework and classwork. At the same time, I also have students who get As on tests and don't do any homework or classwork. They could end up failing because the emphasis is really to put more on the day-to-day work that they're supposed to be doing." Thus, Mr. Larken's grading system awarded not only student learning, but also specific academic behaviors he thought were important: turning in homework and finishing assignments.

Ms. Phillips, a 2nd-year biology teacher at Alexander, had a slightly different approach to grading. She also emphasized the importance of doing work in class, but she put less emphasis on homework. After "killing myself just grading everything" the previous year, she decided to reserve her thoughtful grading for "assessment-type projects, papers, and tests." But for "a lot of stuff we'll do in class, I'll go around and just check off if they have it or not, and they get full credit. So it's like 20 points. They get 20 out of 20" for much of their daily work in class. "It's like a test would be 100 and that's a lot of points, and daily work is like 20 or 30 points." Besides its efficiency, the advantage of this system was that it was "a great way to reward the kids who come to school and do their class work but never do any homework or don't study." She found this to be a good way to, "I don't want to say 'pad their grades,' but like, when I was grading everything if it was right or wrong, then everyone was getting Fs." Ms. Phillips's new grading system was "just rewarding effort."

Alexander High literature teacher Ms. Orozco was motivated by similar impulses. She recognized that many students had difficult lives outside of school and often didn't do homework, so she said she "gives lots of points during the day" to motivate them to participate and complete work in class, because "students are very interested in points." She thought giving students points for participation helped them "feel successful."

Ms. Orozco spoke in generalities about three different groups of students: the highest achievers, the ones who didn't really come to school, and the large group in the middle. Ms. Orozco believed students had already sorted themselves into these different levels of achievement—"kids have decided what grade they believe they will get before they come into my class"—and had tried to devise reasonable strategies for the two groups of students who were still coming to school. Ms. Orozco was aware that ultimately her top students would be competing against students in the suburbs for college admission, so "an A here should be the same as an A in the suburbs." She did not give many As.

On the other hand, she said, "a C just means average," so Cs should be more attainable. With her strategy for awarding daily points, students could earn a C even if they were struggling with the skills she was trying to teach. On major projects, which made up about half the total grade each quarter, she told students that "if you do the project you will get a C." She balanced this against points for classwork, so students who regularly came to class but did not perform well on the major project could still pass. Given this system, "the only kids who fail my class are kids that don't come to school."

Each of the teachers at Alexander had a reasoned approach to assigning grades. They tried to negotiate the tension between maintaining professional standards—comparing assignments and grades to what students "3 miles down the street" in the wealthy suburbs would be exposed—and recognizing the academic backgrounds and behaviors of their own students, who often "didn't do homework" or "just wanted to pass the class" with a low grade. They were cognizant of the importance of motivating students, and they used their point system as a primary form of extrinsic motivation. Clearly, Alexander teachers had designed grading policies they thought were in the best interests of the students in front of them.

From the perspective of Alexander students, however, grading was often an opaque and random process over which they seemed to feel little power or control. Each teacher had a different approach to weighting assignments, and the relationship between a student's work and her course grade was often unclear. Students often explained their current grades by relaying to me whatever their teachers most recently told them about their performance. For example, Monique was trying to explain how her grade in one class dropped suddenly from an A to an F. "[I had] missing assignments and then, um, my binder that I have for her class, she said that some of my stuff wasn't in there and then she said some of it wasn't completed and stuff." Apparently, this moved Monique from earning an A to failing the class. When I queried Shana about how she was graded on work in Mr. Larken's history class, she started laughing and shaking her head. "I don't know how he do it. I don't know how he grades."

Ability and Competence Grow with Effort: Grading in Devon High School

Devon High used a fundamentally different system for determining grades and credits, one in which grades were tied directly to students' efforts and increased competence. Grades at Devon were based on demonstrated learning rather than an averaging of points across a semester. Devon teachers specified learning outcomes for each course (e.g., "Uses evidence from multiple, historical primary sources to support a position") and then used student work to determine whether or not students met each outcome. For a year-long course, teachers would assess students on perhaps 30–35 learning outcomes in total. Rather than receiving points on assignments or a final letter grade for their work in an entire course, students were rated on each individual learning outcome using ratings of *Proficient* (P), *High Performance* (HP), or *Not Yet Proficient* (NY). To pass a course and receive credit, students needed to demonstrate proficiency (a rating of *P* or *HP*) on at least 70% of the outcomes for that course. Students were considered "failing" if more than 30% of assessed course outcomes were rated as *Not Yet*. Thus, Devon students never actually received Fs. Instead, they were told they were *Not Yet Proficient* in specific outcomes and expected to put in more work until they reached proficiency.

Where students in Maxwell and Alexander needed to earn at least 60% of the total possible points to pass a class regardless of what they actually learned (60% = D–), students in Devon passed classes by demonstrating they had learned at least 70% of the key material at a *Proficient* level or better.

Devon students could all articulate the meaning of the three different outcome ratings. As Alisha explained: "*High Performance*, it's like you doing good, like real good. And *Proficient* is, you doing good, but it's okay. And *Not Yet* is that you just need to bring your grades up." Tiffany described it similarly: "*HP* is *High Performance*. It mean you did real good, it's like an A. *Proficient* [means] you did good but you could have did a little bit better. It's like a B. And *NY* is not really failing, so I can't say it's like a D or F. Maybe like a C? Like, you know a little bit of it, but you don't know as much as you should know, or you need to work on it some more."

Juana pointed to Devon teachers' widespread use of rubrics as an aid to helping her understand her grades. She knew how she earned each grade because "the teacher gives comments, but we have a little rubric that shows us *P, HP, Not Yet*, what we have to do to get all of those. So you have to go by [the rubric] while you're doing the project. And if you [deserve] all *HPs*, then the teacher look at it and circle *HPs*" on the rubric.

The teachers and administrators who designed Devon's assessment system specifically tried to create an approach to student evaluation that would take the negative charge out of failure. Even the term *"Not Yet"* seemed to frame failed efforts in a much more palatable light—and to directly suggest that more effort was necessary to learn more. This was reflected in Tiffany's comment about her experience of grades at Devon: "Sometimes you do your work . . . but sometimes it's just not right. So they just put a *NY* on it, which means you just need to work on it some more." Rather than deflating her, Juana said when she received a *Not Yet*, "it kinda . . . propels me cause I want better, so I try to redo the assignment, get it better, give it back" for a higher rating.

The second big difference in Devon's grading system was that, even after a course ended and grades were posted on transcripts, they could be changed if students demonstrated additional learning. If Devon students failed a course—meaning they had not met the minimum threshold of 70% of the outcomes by the end of the course, they were expected to do remediation work to meet additional outcomes. When a student could demonstrate proficiency in a previously unmet outcome, her teacher would change the student's official rating on that outcome (e.g., from *Not Yet* to *Proficient*). Once a student met 70% of the course outcomes this way, she received credit for the course. Any teacher who saw evidence of more work and more learning could change the rating on any outcome, allowing for maximum flexibility in how and when students "made up" their past *Not Yets*.

Tiffany explained that "you can go to your teachers, and ask them what do I need to work on, what I'm missing, and they'll let you know." Once students do this additional work, "all we have to do is go to the teacher and be like, 'Here's our work that we got a *Not Yet* on. Can you change it?' And they'll see that we did it, and if it's a *P* or if it's higher than a *NY*, then they'll go in the computer and change" the rating. Tiffany noted she could do more work and change an outcome "even if it's [already] on your report card." Thus, course credit was not tied to getting at least a D within a semester's time, but rather to attaining a level of mastery of specified learning outcomes for the course, regardless of the time it took to do so.

Because every student could raise their grades at Devon—even strong students could change *Proficient* ratings to *High Performance*—the act of working on *Not Yets* or redoing work on past outcomes became normalized.

When everyone was engaged in improving their performance, students didn't feel penalized by it. Tiffany noted that "if I get an *NY*, sometimes I just be, like, oh, I'll make it up later. But if it's something that I really need to work on, then I tell my friends 'I can't talk 'til I get this *NY* off.'"

Under this grading structure, students' relationship to their own evaluation seemed markedly different from the experience of Alexander students. Brittany explained that if a student wanted to check on her grades, "You go on the high school website and you type in your [login], and it all pops up." Students were able to go online to the school's Student Evaluation system to see their current status in each class (the percentage of course outcomes they had met to date with at least a *Proficient* rating). Latrice said she knew her exact percentages in each class "right now" because "I check my percentage every day." Students could also print out a list of outcomes rated as *Not Yet* from all current or previous classes. Brittany said that "every time I make up an assignment, I look at [the online system] so I can check it off that I already did it." She said she checked all her classes online every week.

Some students at Devon did have to repeat classes. When students met very few course outcomes after a full year of instruction, they were required to retake the class on the premise that it would be unreasonable to expect them to make much independent progress without the benefit of daily support from a teacher. Devon principal Dr. Antonia explained the philosophy undergirding this policy:

> Having to repeat a course [under any grading system] is a function of not being successful enough to learn like more than half the material. Our basic structural premise is if you can learn half of the material—and we require 70% of the knowledge to be demonstrated to get the credit—that you live in this netherworld between, "I know more than half, so I shouldn't have to start at ground zero, but I don't know enough to be acknowledged as knowing enough to get credits." And so that's really the contested area. And that's really where I think failure in the traditional sense of grading systems is immoral.

Students who failed a class but had a demonstrated grasp of the course material were able to do more work and provide additional evidence of their learning without retaking the course. In essence, the system acknowledged what they had already learned but held them accountable for making up the gap between what they knew and some established threshold (70% of the material) to earn course credit. Students who finished a course with very little understanding were required to take the course again the next school year.

This points to a third important difference with Devon's system. Students could turn in work at any time (even years after a course ended) to demonstrate their proficiency in an outcome. Though all work had due dates and students were badgered and cajoled into trying to meet them, students suffered no grading penalty for late work. This made "procrastination" a topic of continual discussion (and often frustration) among Devon teachers, but turning in work late did not hamper students' efforts to improve their grades and pass classes.

LATE WORK POLICIES MAKE IT DIFFICULT TO CATCH UP

Part of the problem students encountered when they tried to catch up in classes at Maxwell or Alexander was that teachers did not give full credit for late work. As was clear from student interviews, much of the work they turned in was late, submitted in hopes of bringing up a low or failing grade. Alexander social studies teacher Mr. Larken described "what's supposed to be a school policy for late work." According to the policy, students were allowed to turn in work from any given unit up to 1 week after the unit test, for up to 75% credit, equivalent to a grade of C. But "if it's a late assignment that's also not done well," Mr. Larken added, "you know, they'll go down" in the grade they earn. It would be reasonable to assume that students struggling to pass classes often received less than maximum credit for late work. An on-time assignment that would have earned a C instead gets an F if it's turned in late. Clearly, trying to improve one's grade by turning in missing assignments past the due date was a futile strategy for pulling out of failure. And yet, that was the only option Maxwell and Alexander students had once they fell behind.

Contrary to the notion of a uniform "late work" policy across all classes at Alexander High, Kendra's experience was that each teacher had his or her own way of handling late work. One teacher "make it hard because you got to have his assignments right on time. If you don't have it in on time, he don't give you no extra time to try to get it in. He put a zero in. And if you put a zero in, your grade go down a lot, for just one zero. And he don't do extra credit work. He don't do none of that." For another teacher, Kendra said, "If you turn something in late, the highest you can get is a C on it. Even if it's really an A, you gonna get a C." And other teachers? "Everybody take off points for it being late," Kendra reported, but each teacher seemed to have a different approach.

Missing and late assignments took a huge toll on Alexander students' grades. Shana dropped from a C to an F in one class because she only "turned half of my project in because I didn't know that we supposed to have turned in a picture with it, and [the missing picture] had dropped my grade down to a F." I asked if she was able to turn in the picture once she realized it was missing. "But, see, when I turned it back in, the picture was late. So it didn't really put points on my grade."

Under Alexander's traditional grading system, students' main strategy to rectify a low or failing grade was to submit late work when and if teachers reminded them about missing assignments. Unfortunately, once students were failing a class, late work that earned no more (and usually much less) than 75% credit was very unlikely to tip the scales on their overall course grade. By significantly discounting the value of late work, teachers made it almost impossible for students to catch up again once they started falling behind.

This fact was often lost on students, however. In the traditional point system, students knew points were good and more points were better, and it seemed as though teachers routinely enticed them with high-point assignments. Monique told me about an upcoming assignment that she hoped would pull her out of a failing grade. She said the teacher was "giving us this project and it's worth 250 points. You know I'm doing it!" Unfortunately, unless students actually earned the full point value on these assignments—in other words, got As on them—the assignments did little to bring up their overall average.

Shana had just turned in a 700-point project in one class which she thought would significantly raise her grade. "Seven hundred points," she repeated. "That's like a A-plus-plus!" She neglected to calculate that 700 more points would also be added to the "points possible" half of the grading equation. Unless she earned a significantly better grade on the large project than she was averaging already in the class, the 700-point project would have no impact on her overall course grade. Students who did not realize this grew increasingly frustrated when their efforts to bring up their grades with new assignments and make up missing assignments did not move them any farther ahead.

Shana was trying to improve a D grade in one of her classes. She had no clear idea how much work she would have to submit to rise above a D. "It seems like, when you turn stuff in, it takes a while for the grade to get up. So, it's like, I've been turning in late work" and waiting to see what would happen, with no sense of the exact relationship between her submission of additional work and anticipated changes in her grade.

"It's Too Late for Me in There"

Other students at Alexander and Maxwell High Schools were well aware that the point system was inherently unforgiving once they had fallen behind. They knew that, somewhere in the marking period, the number of points remaining to be earned would not be large enough to get them up to the 60% required to pass; the time limit to earn a passing grade expired well before the course actually ended. Each Maxwell and Alexander student I interviewed said they had already given up trying to pass at least one current class, even though there were still many months left in the semester. In comparison, none of the Devon students expressed the idea of being too far gone for hope, even in classes they were failing.

Consider this discussion with Dawson about his year-long freshman biology class at Maxwell, which he failed in fall semester "'cause I barely went." He realized skipping class "wasn't a good thing" and in February began attending and doing "D average" work, but by then "it was too late to come back to do enough." When he got his second semester report card, he had failed biology again.

Sonia explained another way it could be "too late" to pass. She said that in "chemistry and geometry I was just like . . . I give up on that. There was no hope in there for me." In March, her chemistry teacher "told me it was too late to catch up on chemistry, so I listened." Though Maxwell offered chemistry tutoring, Sonia didn't bother to go; her teacher's comment convinced her it would be futile. I asked Sonia to clarify the idea of being "too late," pointing out she still had April, May, and part of June left in the course. Why could she not pass chemistry when she was only halfway through the semester? Sonia explained, "Chemistry, it seem like, everything she teaching is something that you had to get at the beginning of the year in order to understand what she teaching now. That's not what it *seems* like, that's what it *is*." Sonia saw no opportunity to learn those beginning building blocks short of retaking the whole year-long course, but she could not start the course over until after she waited several more months to fail the current semester. All she could do now was mark time and then try again next fall.

Dawson pointed out that if a student had a prolonged absence, it would be very hard to return to class. "A kid will be failing and they be like, well, I can't just show up at a class now, after I been gone for like 3 months or something. Then the kid try to show up and try to do his work, but it ain't gonna do nothing, he just gonna fail. So he be thinking in the back of his head, like, there ain't nothing else to do now, I can't pass." Again, the only option was to wait, fail, and start again later.

Students at Alexander and Maxwell had been graded with the same point and letter grade system every year for at least a decade. Despite some inherent problems, they were amazingly uncritical of the system that largely determined their educational fates. In talking with students trying to negotiate their performance in this traditional grading system, I was continually reminded of the saying that fish are the last to discover water. Earning points for work was such a ubiquitous part of their schooling experience that they scarcely thought to question it.

Another striking thing about my interviews with Alexander and Maxwell students was how seldom they seemed to use their teachers as a re-
source in attempting to improve their grades. This was particularly true
if students did not see the teacher as supportive and caring. But even with
teachers they liked, students seemed reticent to seek them out for information about the status of their work or their grades, or to ask for help with
assignments or course material they did not understand.

For example, Shana thought she was getting a D in one of her classes,
and to bring up her grade she would have to complete "the project I for-
got to turn in." I asked if she knew how to do the project. "Nope," which
she said was why she had not done it. Because she did not know how to
approach the missing work, Shana seemed to conclude that she could do
nothing further to improve her grade. Students appeared to have developed a striking passivity in relation to grades, as though it were something
being done to them by mysterious forces over which they had little influence. Grading practices varied from teacher to teacher, and the criteria by
which any given teacher determined final grades were unclear to students.
Even when students put in the effort to turn in late work and complete
missing assignments, these had little impact on their grades. The whole
system seemed to reinforce students' sense of not being in control of their
own academic fates.

This was in sharp contrast to students at Devon High, who all spoke
repeatedly about seeking out help from their teachers to improve their performance. Alisha explained how Devon's grading system encouraged this.
When students got *Not Yets*, "You gotta make them up. You gotta go to
the teacher and they tell you what you got to do. And if you already know
how to do it, and you show them you know how to do it, they'll just take
[the *Not Yet* rating] off" and replace it with a higher rating (*Proficient* or
High Performance). If she did not already know how to do the work, Alisha said, "Then [the teacher is] gonna give you some work and help you
with stuff." Students were expected to seek out their teachers to discuss
any outcomes with *Not Yet* ratings and find out what they needed to do to
improve their performance.

Sharday echoed these sentiments about going to teachers for help at
Devon. Teachers "will explain it to you. . . . If you get a *Not Yet*, they will
help you on it and everything." Juana said that if she felt herself falling behind, "I feel like I can ask" people in her school for help. She laughed, "My
teachers are totally talkable to." Having observed closely and interviewed
students and teachers in both schools, I don't think that teachers were any
more approachable at Devon. The school just utilized a system that required
students to be in ongoing communication with their teachers about their
academic performance.

Tiffany described how Devon's report card format also helped her understand how she was doing in her classes. Rather than the traditional CPS letter grade report card, students got a whole "packet" of information. "We actually have comments from your teachers, like they say, 'You did good in this but you need to work on this,' and then it has a list of outcomes that you need to work on." Courtney also appreciated Devon's report card, "'cause [teachers] could write like little notes on the report cards . . . and like, basically all of them told me, 'I know you can do better, you just got to put in the effort. I know you know the stuff but you just don't do it.'" Courtney said, "It makes me feel better if the notes are in there because sometimes, if you do improve, you get compliments on that, like, 'I knew you could do it' or whatever, 'See, you just got to put your head into it and just try.'"

Latrice also felt a sense of control over her grades at Devon. On most assignments, she said, "I try to get a *HP*, but if it's worth the *P* then I just take that, as long as it's not a *Not Yet*." She was satisfied with a *P* "most of the time. It's like if it's something that I know I can like, ace it, I do it over for the *HP*," noting she had earned *HP*s on all but three humanities assignments that year.

A Devon science teacher thought the assessment system worked particularly well for students "who have the ability to plan." She described one student who asked her teachers about their policies on making up *Not Yet*s and then used that information to figure out how to allocate her effort on assignments. The student apparently knew how many *Not Yet*s she could reasonably make up within the marking period and which teachers would allow her to raise a rating from a *Not Yet* to a *High Performance*. The science teacher said this student "had like four *Not Yet*s the whole entire year, and she planned each one of those *Not Yet*s. She knew she was going to get them, and she wasn't upset about them." The student figured out it was better to concentrate on getting *High Performances* from certain teachers initially, and she could next turn her attention to assignments where she could earn *High Performance* through make-up work. Although this allowed for a lot of student control, the science teacher thought this was most beneficial for students who "had the foresight" to plan ahead. Other students, she lamented, would pile up too many *Not Yet*s within a term and then be unable to complete all their work.

I was particularly interested in how enthusiastic Brittany was about the grading system at Devon, given that she had been there almost 2 years and was still repeating all her 9th-grade classes. In comparing Devon to a regular public high school, she said students learned more at Devon because of the teachers. Brittany interpreted Devon's alternative grading system as a sign that "the teachers care. At [traditional] public school they just give you work; they don't care if you do it or not. If you fail, you fail." In contrast, she said, teachers at Devon "make you want to learn. . . . They let you make your work up. Like in public school, if you get an F, you just got an F. But here, if you get an F—well, a *Not Yet*—they let you make it up and then you can change your grade. . . . They can give you chances to make it up, and after a while you just do it."

<h2 style="text-align:center">CRITIQUES OF GRADING IN
MAXWELL HIGH SCHOOL CLASSROOMS</h2>

Though I did not ask Maxwell students about grading practices directly, they talked about their grades and remediation efforts when describing classes they failed. Dawson complained that it was hard to get access to teachers outside of the classroom to get academic help. He thought the school should employ more "assistants" who could "help kids" both during and outside of class. "Sometimes we got free periods, and some kids, like, will want to go and talk to their teacher or something. But we can't get out the lunch room 'cause they won't let us."

Rodney offered a thoughtful critique of the traditional grading system by which he was evaluated at Maxwell. Although he believed "grades are important," he went on to say that he thought students shouldn't get grades "because it don't do nothing. . . . On paper, it shows your progress but . . . people try to learn . . . and like, you probably know something. But if you don't put it into words, you get a bad grade, but you still, like, [have] the information. That's why I feel like we shouldn't get grades. We should just get a pass or fail, instead of grades." I asked him if he thought students worked harder because they knew they'd be graded. "No," he replied. "because . . . like me, I found out I had an F in chemistry. Like, I been doing well on all my tests and quizzes. I haven't been turning in my homework; that's what get me the F. But when I first saw my F I'm like, I did all that, all that over-the-night studying for these quizzes and tests, and I still received an F. . . . Why should I work harder?"

<h2 style="text-align:center">COMPARING STUDENT EXPERIENCES IN
GRADING SYSTEMS ACROSS THREE SCHOOLS</h2>

In contrast to their peers at Alexander and Maxwell, students at Devon seemed to feel very much in control of their grades and understood the process by which they would pass classes. Students were able to access teachers outside of class for help and guidance, and they reported taking advantage of these opportunities as standard practice in trying to pass courses. Because late work counted for "full credit" in meeting course out-comes, Devon students felt as though they were able to make discernible progress in improving their course performance, even if they were coming from far behind. They saw that their ability and competence grew with their effort—and their grades improved accordingly. The availability of structured opportunities to work directly with teachers on missing work to improve their grades had a profound impact on students' classroom experiences and expectations of their own success. As Diamond put it, "It was like somebody was behind me."

Because Devon students were both able and expected to make up *Not Yets* during the regular academic year, they didn't have to wait until they failed a course to do remediation. This was one of the main things Tiffany liked about Devon's grading system: "They give you a lot of chances to make up your work." She continued: "If I was going to a [regular] public school and I missed an assignment, they would just give you an F, just off the bat, an F. But if I miss an assignment here, they give you an *NY*. . . . It is real good. 'Cause I be busy a lot, so sometimes I don't have time to do the work, but then I have time to make it up, so I just make it up." This reminded me of something Dawson said about Maxwell High School. I had asked him if course grades were accurate reflections of what students actually know. "No," he told me, poor grades "could mean [students are] just, they're not learning fast enough. But they know how to do the work. You gotta give a kid the chance to do what they do. You gotta give 'em their little space so you can see what they really know."

Devon students felt more hopeful about their academic success than students at Maxwell or Alexander, which they attributed directly to school structures that supported their achievement. Sharday summarized her inter-pretation of how Devon promoted student success:

> This the only school I know that help you with your work, get you after-school programs. . . . If they give you all this extra space, all this extra time, it ain't no way that you can't do it. . . .This school gives more than two chances. Everybody say the third time should be right. They give you more than two or three chances. And I don't see how you couldn't be able to pass.

In contrast, Alexander and Maxwell students were skeptical and discour-aged about their ability to catch up with their peers and graduate on time, as grading practices and late work policies seemed to thwart them at every turn.

In comparing the grading systems in Alexander, Maxwell, and Devon High Schools, key differences emerged on each of the four dimensions of student achievement. The first was a structural difference in the way grading systems interacted with students' efforts to "catch up" in their classes. Across all three schools, students who ended up failing a course usually fell behind due to a combination of missing work and low grades on work they'd completed. Policies at Maxwell and Alexander often made it impossible for students to recover once they got behind, because turning in late work did not yield high enough point values to improve their failing grades. The mechanisms used to stratify achievement by leveraging differences in student learning—points and letter grades that distinguished the "top of the class" from everybody else—were exactly the mechanisms that produced academic failure and impeded recovery. Devon's grading system allowed students to go back and demonstrate their learning at any time without penalty. As a result, even though Devon students actually fell behind at greater rates than students in the two traditional schools, they were more often able to catch up and pass classes. Students at Alexander and Maxwell, on the other hand, found that it was sometimes "too late" for them to pass current classes; they had to wait until the end of the term to fail, and then start over again in another term.

Second, on the academic dimension, grading systems differed in the usefulness of the feedback they generated about students' course performance. Devon's assessment system provided students with useful, actionable information on their performance that not only helped them to master material, but also reinforced feelings of self-efficacy and control over their fate. Devon students knew exactly which piece of knowledge or which skill they needed to develop in order to raise their grade, allowing them to focus on learning that piece. Conversely, the traditional grading system at Maxwell and Alexander seemed to provide much more opaque information that obscured students' understanding of the relationship between their grades and their academic mastery. It seemed that the way to improve one's grade was to build up a higher stack of work, with no clear connection to specific knowledge or skills. Demonstration of learning in one mode (for example, homework) was more valued than demonstration of the same learning in a different mode (for example, on a test), but the valued mode differed for each teacher. As a result of these differences across the three schools, Devon students who fell behind in a course were more successful in remediating their learning and catching up again. Once Alexander and Maxwell students fell behind, they were much less likely to earn a passing grade.

Third, on the developmental dimension, the two grading systems provided very different mechanisms and incentives for helping students develop a sense of responsibility for their work or a habit of seeking help from teachers. Students at Devon were required to complete missing work or redo low-quality work until it met the standards set by their teachers. Students had to communicate with their teachers about what they knew and didn't know and produce work that demonstrated their knowledge and skills. In contrast, students at Maxwell and Alexander seldom sought out their teachers for help, other than to get lists of their missing assignments. If they turned in low-quality work, that work was simply graded down. Students were not required—or even allowed—to rectify errors or put in additional effort once an assignment was submitted and graded. As a result, Devon students began developing habits and strategies for improving their performance, while Alexander and Maxwell students seemed to be learning how to passively await their own failure.

Finally, the two grading systems functioned very differently on the motivational dimension. Devon students saw a clear connection between work and reward: Concerted effort almost invariably produced a passing grade, even when students were starting from way behind. Hard work actually paid off. This motivated students at Devon to continue trying until they reached the threshold required to pass the course. In contrast, students at Maxwell and Alexander experienced diminishing returns as their late work yielded too few points to change their overall grade. Eventually, most of these students gave up trying to catch up. They had to wait out the remainder of the semester until they could fail the course and start over again. As they got older and their peers got closer to graduation, students grew increasingly bitter and disheartened about these idle, wasted months.

Taken together, the grading system at Devon High School seemed better aligned to support the academic, developmental, and motivational needs of students. The structural components of the school's competency-based system made it clear to students what they were supposed to be learning (expressed as course outcomes), enabled them to understand the quality of their performance relative to the learning goal (based on how they were rated on each outcome), provided multiple opportunities and teacher support to improve their performance, and created motivational conditions that encouraged students' ongoing efforts.

In contrast, the grading system at Alexander and Maxwell High Schools worked at cross-purposes with students' academic, developmental, and motivational needs. The structural components of the traditional points and letter grades system served to obscure both the goals of learning (whereby earning points became the de facto goal) and the relationship between hard work and improvement (by discounting the value of work at different points in time). Students rarely if ever got feedback on what they were learning or the quality of their understanding; instead, their teachers were almost entirely focused on what assignments they had or had not completed. Perhaps most important, the two schools' traditional grading system seemed to undermine student motivation. When students' repeated efforts didn't pay, students stopped trying to pass their classes.

SEVEN

Credits Are No Joke

Remediation and Recovery Structures Across Three Schools

In the last chapter we saw how differences in grading systems affected students' efforts to catch up when they fell behind in their classes. Traditional grading practices based on point averages, time-based marking periods (semesters), and late work policies combined to constrain the achievement windows for students at Maxwell and Alexander. If they had not earned at least 60% of the possible points in a class by semester's end, students got an F on their transcript, putting them a half-credit behind in credits for graduation. Though Devon had a more forgiving system, if students there had not met at least 70% of course outcomes by the end of a term, they likewise failed to earn course credit. Across the three schools, all 14 students experienced multiple course failures, meaning they needed to "recover" these lost course credits to make progress toward their diplomas.

I did not have complete transcript data for students in Study 1, but this will give a sense of what was happening with the eight students at Alexander and Devon in Study 2: On average, these students took a typical load of between seven and eight courses per term, which would have yielded seven or eight credits per year if they passed all their classes. By the end of their second year of high school (June 2008), students should have each accumulated a total of about 15 credits toward the 24 required for graduation. Instead, study participants were failing roughly half the courses they attempted. They earned just below 4 credits per year on average, totaling an average 7.9 credits after 2 years, ranging from an individual low of 2.5 to a high of 12.5 by June 2008.

Importantly, most students in Study 2 (seven of the eight) failed more classes per term as time went on, effectively losing credits at a faster pace. (Brittany was the exception; she failed all her classes in freshman year, and improved that the following year by earning 2.5 credits.) On average, the eight students lost 3.9 credits in freshman year and 5.25 credits in sophomore year.

Interestingly, Devon students in my small sample actually failed more classes than students at Alexander, despite strong support at Devon and greater ability for students who had fallen behind in a class to catch up. At first, this didn't make any sense to me, seeming to conflict with what students in the two schools were saying about the relative ease or difficulty of catching up from behind across the different grading systems. But as I talked with teachers and observed what was happening with the students in Study 2, it became clear that the stakes of failure were so much lower at Devon that teachers were more willing to fail students if they were not satisfied with their level of learning. Remember that failure at Devon simply meant students had "not yet" demonstrated sufficient learning to get credit for the course by the end of the term; there was no time limit on a student's ability to rectify this and earn retroactive credit. Once a student earned the credit, all evidence of "failure" was removed from her transcript and replaced with evidence of her accomplishment. Failure had no long-term consequences at Devon.

Conversely, teachers at Alexander recognized that course failure was a huge detriment to their students, with every failure substantially increasing students' likelihood of dropping out of school. Fs stayed permanently on student transcripts and hurt students' GPAs. Course credits seemed much more difficult to make up, as students had to retake entire classes. As was evident in their point systems, teachers at Alexander tried to manipulate the system every way they could to allow students to pass courses, even if they hadn't adequately learned the material. Failure in the traditional system seemed to be something to avoid at all costs, if at all possible.

In this light, the higher failure rate at Devon made sense. The stakes of failure were much lower for students, and as a result, teachers could hold students to higher standards to pass a course. As this chapter will illustrate, though Devon students in my small sample failed more classes than Alexander students, most Devon students also recovered credits more quickly, ultimately earning more credits toward graduation than their peers in the traditional high school.

REMEDIATION, CREDIT RECOVERY, AND
FOUR DIMENSIONS OF STUDENT ACHIEVEMENT

The grade pattern of increasing failures over time demonstrated by 13 of the 14 students is typical of young people in the process of dropping out of high school, and it stands to reason: Academic failure undermines student motivation, and lower motivation contributes to further failure. It is also "commonsensical" in that 9th-graders who did not learn enough to pass freshman classes would not have the requisite knowledge and skills to do well academically in 10th grade. This is failure's snowballing effect. In addition, if students didn't develop effective strategies to address the problems that led to their failure in the first place, there is little reason to believe their performance would miraculously improve in subsequent semesters, despite their best hopes and earnest resolves to change.

Barring some interruption to this pattern, it should be no surprise that students across all three schools who failed classes early in high school would likely continue to fail as time went on. Differences in grading and credit systems across schools did not seem to prevent course failure. Using the earlier analogy to international poverty, students were losing credits and falling *into* failure at roughly similar rates across schools. The question then is whether a different grading and credit system could change the rate at which students recovered credits to get *out* of failure.

To get failing students out of failure, remediation and recovery efforts have to address the structural, academic, developmental, and motivational dimensions of student achievement. On the most basic structural level, failing students need opportunities for both remediation and recovery. I use the word *remediation* for opportunities *while a course is still in session* for students to learn the material or develop the skills they haven't mastered, so they can finish the class with a passing grade. In most Chicago high schools, optional after-school tutoring tended to be the default remediation strategy.

If remediation is unsuccessful—in other words, once students fail a course—they need to somehow recover credit for the class to advance toward graduation. *Recovery* refers to opportunities both to learn course material and to earn lost course credit *after a class has already ended*. The recovery strategy used by most CPS high schools was to have students retake failed courses through evening classes or in summer school.

This chapter looks closely at the structured opportunities made available to Alexander, Maxwell, and Devon students for remediation and credit recovery and examines how well these structured opportunities addressed the academic, developmental, and motivational dimensions of student achievement. We will also look at how students responded to available opportunities and what ultimately happened when they pursued the paths laid out for them.

I did not investigate remediation and recovery opportunities in Study 1 except as the topic arose naturally in student interviews, so I don't know the full extent of remediation options available at Maxwell High School. Students there told me that teachers offered after-school tutoring in several subjects, and administrators were proactive in directing students to summer school and evening classes to recover credits from failed courses. I looked at remediation and recovery opportunities much more closely in Study 2 through interviews with students, teachers, principals, and counselors at Devon and Alexander High Schools.

Structuring Remediation and Recovery

All 14 students in my studies resolved to do better after they failed courses in freshman year. All three schools recognized that credit deficiency put students at great risk of dropping out of school, and school staff acted swiftly to get failing students on the path to credit recovery. And yet, there were clear differences between schools in the effectiveness of everyone's efforts. For each of the three schools, I describe how remediation and recovery opportunities were structured and how students participated, then look at the academic, motivational, and developmental dimensions of students' experiences within these structures.

Night School and Summer School at Maxwell High. Maxwell High School actively steered students to night school and summer school for credit recovery, though none of the Maxwell students in Study 1 initially availed themselves of summer school options. As Dawson put it, "That's why I end up messing up, right there, cause I didn't go to summer school." Instead, after an unexpectedly demoralizing 1st year of high school, he just wanted a break. "Like for my summer, I felt like I was free. I didn't have to go to do no work, I hang outside every day." Of course, that meant in Dawson's second year of high school he was constantly playing catch-up as he tried to earn back missing credits. Rodney's family went to Memphis during summer after his freshman year, which meant that he didn't attend summer school either. Sonia also hadn't gone to summer school after 9th grade "because we had moved out to the suburbs. . . . I had no way to [get to] the city all summer."

Though none of my Maxwell students went to summer school after freshman year, all three had plans to participate in night school, although Rodney was the only one who was already attending a recovery class (on Saturdays). By spring of their 2nd year, all three Maxwell students were making elaborate plans to recover credits lost to failure. My conversations with them generally went like this one with Dawson. We were talking about a double-period algebra course he failed in 9th grade, and I asked how he was going to make up the math credit.

> *Dawson*: Well, since it's a double period, it's kind of one whole credit, so I can just go to summer school and take that class, and then I can take two classes actually in summer school 'cause they only allow you to take two.
>
> *Q*: This coming summer?
>
> *Dawson*: Right. So hopefully I can take my double-period algebra, and my biology, so that's one [more] half-credit right there, so I can get

that out the way. Then the following year I'm going to take night school and make up these classes right now, like geometry, that I'm messing up in.

Dawson was currently failing both geometry and American Literature in that spring semester.

Q: Okay. So if you end up failing those classes, you could . . .
Dawson: . . . take night school . . .
Q: . . . and make it up. And when would you do that?
Dawson: Next semester, 'cause this semester, night school about to be over with anyway.
Q: So it would be next year to make those up. And in summer school you'd do algebra and biology?
Dawson: Right, I'd do summer school this year and do them two classes and get them out the way. . . . Well, really I can go to two different schools to make up all four of these classes.
Q: What do you mean? Tell me about that.
Dawson: All these schools, you limited to two classes in the summer schools, but if I take my two classes here and, 'cause summer school end about 12 [noon], then I could go to another school and take night school right now, take my other two classes to make up. And then show my stuff over here [back at Maxwell], that I did it.

If he were to have any chance of getting back on track to graduate with his peers, Dawson would have had to attend two classes in summer school and two more in night school over the summer, then the following year attend evening school at two different high schools, while meanwhile passing all of his classes in regular school—something he had not yet done in his four semesters of high school.

Rodney was making similar plans. Now in spring of his 2nd year, he was taking a Saturday recovery class to earn an algebra credit. He had already been attending class on Saturday mornings for 6 weeks, and he had 4 more weeks to go. And then, "I'm going to apply for night school, when we come back off a spring break."

For the summer following Sonia's 2nd year at Maxwell, she was planning to go to summer school to earn geometry and chemistry credits. And "night school, okay, I think there's four sessions of night school, and one just passed, one is over, and when we come back from spring break that's when another one [starts]. That's the last one; I'm gonna take that one. I'm gonna probably do PE or something, health or something." Though she had several courses she needed to make up, she would have to find some other way to recover her other credits, because "I think you can only take one class at night school." Sonia had only earned two credits by spring of her second year. I asked her, realistically, what's the plan? "Okay, the plan is to get as close to 15 as I can." I helped her count the credits she could earn:

> *Q:* So if you pass [a semester each of] U.S. history, American literature, Spanish, and art, then you'll get two more credits, right? You'll get half for each of those. So then you'll have four [total]. And then, you go to . . .
>
> *Sonia:* . . . summer school.
>
> *Q:* And so for night school you can get . . .
>
> *Sonia:* . . . like a half.
>
> *Q:* Okay, a half, and then for summer school you can get . . .
>
> *Sonia:* A whole credit.
>
> *Q:* Ok, so that's five and a half. Do you think five and a half is what you'll have by fall?
>
> *Sonia:* Mmm . . . yeah. [pause] And then I'm only be a sophomore. So I got to do the whole night school thing over. . . . But then if I go do another school for summer school, they give us two whole credits, so I'm thinking about going to [another school] for that. . . . I think you have to go for the whole summer.
>
> *Q:* So then next year, to catch back up, you would need to—what?— pass all your classes and . . .
>
> *Sonia:* Do some night school. I'm a do the night school every semester next year.

I asked Sonia what she saw when she looked toward the future. How did she picture herself at 25 years old? "I see me on my own . . . not *trying* to make a way, but *making* a way." She said the most important thing to getting there was "just, right now. School." She felt like that was important, "just, it's hard, trying to get them credits. Credits are no joke."

Tutoring at Alexander High School. Alexander's primary remediation strategy was to offer after-school tutoring to students who wanted extra help. In walking through the halls at Alexander, I counted 13 different posters distributed throughout three floors of the building, advertising regularly scheduled (e.g., Wednesdays and Thursdays from 2:30 to 3:30) after-school tutoring in math, science, language arts, and social studies at designated classroom "learning centers," as well as an after-school writing lab. Despite these concerted efforts, however, my interview data indicated that tutoring services were underutilized by failing students. According to one teacher, "It started off pretty well. We had peer tutors that were in here, [but that] died after first semester. I don't know if the other [teachers] still have theirs going. I'd be surprised. . . . And now it's just kids come in the classroom to do their work after school and I'll help them if they ask me for stuff, but it's pretty informal now." Nevertheless, he said, "there's [students] there every day, especially now, once projects are due."

Ms. Jenkins, the principal at Alexander High, provided further background information on the school's tutoring efforts. "Every department does their own tutoring and it's not mandatory. We've had every version of tutoring in this building and none of them are successful. I don't know if any school" has a successful program. Though she thought tutoring services worked for a particular niche of students who just needed a little extra help or attention to succeed, she felt tutoring was less utilized by students with more significant levels of course failure.

Shana was the only one of the three Alexander students who talked about going to tutoring. She raised her freshman algebra grade from a D to a C because her algebra teacher "was sitting down talking to me and all that type of stuff. She was helping me. She got me tutors. And, you know, I came to the math learning center. She had helped me." Shana also worked with her science teacher during daily advisory periods on days when she was late to school and missed his morning class.

Kendra was aware of after-school tutoring at Alexander, but said she never even thought about going. I asked if tutoring might be helpful. "No," she said, "because I know how to do the work. I just got to apply myself." Over the course of five interviews with Alexander students, the references cited above were the only instances when students mentioned tutoring services available at the school, even though I asked them specifically about strategies or services to help them do better in their classes.

Night School at Alexander High. Alexander High School administrators and staff were aggressive in getting 9th-graders enrolled in "night school" as soon as they failed any classes. Both Monique and Shana said their counselors told them about night school and gave them applications. Shana added that her principal "Ms. Jenkins actually pulled me out of class. She do not want me to be off-track. So she pulled me out of class, told me I had to go to night school."

Ms. Jenkins confirmed this as the school's primary credit recovery strategy: "If [students] fail at the semester, they're automatically routed to the counselor to sign up for credit recovery. . . . We want them to sign up for night school so that they can make up those credits before the end of the 10th grade. Because it's a slippery slope, and once they start missing classes, it's hard to catch back up." By channeling students immediately to night school instead of waiting until summer or the following year, Alexander counselors were hoping to accelerate the rate at which students recovered credits and got back on track to graduation.

Due to district budget constraints, night classes were only offered at selected CPS high schools, and students were limited in the number of recovery courses they could take at any given school in any given term. As a result, after a full day of school, Alexander students traveled (generally by public transportation) to high schools in other parts of the city for another several hours of class. If they needed to recover credits from several failed courses, they likely traveled to multiple high schools. Shana was attending night school every Wednesday and Friday from 3:30 to 7:30 P.M. at one high school, and then every Tuesday and Thursday at another high school from 6:00 to 7:45 P.M. On top of full-time school at Alexander during the day, "it's a lot," she said.

Academic Workshop and Summer School at Devon High School. Devon High School offered "academic workshops" after school every Tuesday and Thursday, as well as Saturday mornings, for both remediation and credit recovery. Teachers were available during these sessions to work one-on-one with students who had either fallen behind in a current class or failed a previous one. Diamond explained:

> Academic workshop is for students who want to make up *Not Yets*. [Depending on] which classes you're failing, you get to choose whichever one you want to do on [Tuesday and Thursday]. It's from 3:30 to 4:30, and we get to work on anything we want to work on. It's like math class, language arts class, whichever one you want to go to. You can go to any teacher that you think can help you understand it better.

Devon teachers were required to offer assistance to students during one of the weekly academic workshop sessions (Tuesday or Thursday after school or Saturday morning), so some subgroup of teachers was available each of the 3 days. Departments tried to coordinate so that at least one teacher from each core subject area was available at each session.

Descriptions of academic workshop at Devon were in sharp contrast to students' references to tutoring services at Alexander High. All eight Devon students reported attending academic workshops and Saturday school as their primary strategy for passing classes. Alisha went after school "to the teacher that's staying . . . and then they'll help you make up your work." She said she was working with teachers in chemistry, language arts, math, and humanities, either after school or on Saturdays. Latrice reported, "I always come to school on Saturday" to work with her math teacher. Brittany said she had gone "Tuesdays and Thursdays" in recent weeks.

The availability of teachers to work with students outside of class, coupled with the structured process whereby students were expected to communicate with teachers, had a profound impact on Devon students' experiences of failure and support. When Alisha commented that her science teacher cared about her, I asked how she knew that. "Because," she said, "she stay after school every day. And . . . most of the teachers don't stay after school every day. They just stay on certain days. If you ask her to stay, she'll stay." Sharday said her math teacher was a good teacher because "she understand where we be coming from." She showed that "by coming to Saturday school when we asked her to."

Juana said that if she had a *Not Yet* on an outcome in any of her current courses, "to make it up" she would "go to academic workshop. You have to talk to your teacher. Your teacher helps you out, and you show that you can do the work, and they remove that *Not Yet*." This strategy seemed to work for students at Devon. Courtney had significantly improved her freshman science grade in a short time by doing work that converted outcomes previously rated as *Not Yet* to ratings of *Proficient* or *High Performance*. She explained that in science she had met only 20% of the outcomes, but by coming to academic workshop she "got that up to like 86% in about 2 weeks."

For credit recovery, Devon students had four options. First, they could attend academic workshop during the regular school year to work on *Not Yets* from previously failed courses. Second, they could do work in their current courses that addressed outcomes from previous courses. For example, if a student failed English because she did not meet some of the writing outcomes, she could address those outcomes as part of her work in the next year's English class; her new teacher could assess her work and change her past year's ratings. Students who only had to meet a few outcomes to pass a previous course tended to use one of these first two strategies to make up credits during the year. Third, students could attend summer school if they failed a core course. Lastly, if they had done really poorly in a course, meeting less than half the course outcomes, students would be scheduled to retake that class the following year.

Devon High School students had a much easier time recovering course credits than students at Maxwell and Alexander. One big difference was the school's student evaluation database, which kept track of each student's unmet outcomes. This allowed Devon to run targeted academic workshops and summer school programs consisting of 2-week mini-courses tailored to the learning needs of individual students. Rather than retaking an entire course, students with similar sets of *Not Yets* could attend summer school for a short period of instruction (anywhere from a few days to 2 weeks) focused on the outcomes they had yet to meet. For example, the biology teacher could offer a summer mini-session on the organization and transfer of genes, targeted at students with *Not Yet*s in genetics outcomes. By organizing instruction around specific sets of competencies for specific students, Devon High School made it faster and easier to recover credits because students weren't required to repeat a full semester of instruction in order to pass a failed course.

During the regular school year, Courtney failed a freshman reading and writing class in spectacular fashion, with virtually no outcomes met. She had to attend a short (2-week) summer school session to remedy her poor performance. Though this was too short a time for her to make up all of her unmet outcomes, she did make significant headway. She said she started summer with "a zero in reading/writing and I raised it up to maybe like a 54," meaning she achieved proficiency in 54% of the course outcomes over the 2-week summer session. That enabled her to earn course credit the following school year after meeting additional outcomes without retaking the course.

Juana had a very similar experience in making up credit for reading and writing. Like Courtney, Juana didn't pass the class during summer school "because my percentage was so low" to begin with, but Juana said she "ended up getting all that I needed" in those 2 weeks to set her up to recover her credit. She met 66% of course outcomes by the end of summer and was able to meet additional outcomes and earn credit for the course shortly after she began her sophomore year.

Devon students believed that their participation in structured remediation and recovery opportunities would lead to success, and they demonstrated that belief through their active attendance in after-school academic workshops and their enrollment in targeted summer school classes. In explaining the Devon system to me, Juana handily summarized the difference between what I had heard from Maxwell and Alexander students and her experience at Devon:

> In a regular high school, if you don't do the work, then they're like, "Okay, whatever." And then at the end they're like, "Okay, you need summer school." But here, it's like, you don't do the work, and they're like, "Okay, you're coming to academic probation," meaning you go there [to academic workshop] and get the work done. Then when [you're] at the end of the school year, they're like, "Okay, have a nice summer!"

Same Structures, Different Purposes:
Advisory Periods and the Power of Language

In addition to structured remediation and recovery opportunities, all three schools utilized an "advisory" or "homeroom" structure as an additional opportunity for student support. Educators at Devon, Alexander, and Maxwell high schools all cared about fostering trusting student-teacher relationships as a means of connecting students to school and providing support for social-emotional and academic growth. They saw this as a critical aspect of remediation and credit recovery for students who were in danger of failing or dropping out. To this end, students were programmed into daily advisory sessions (called "divisions" at Maxwell and Alexander) according to grade level. Within this schoolwide structure, all three schools had created special groupings of failed students—those who were "in between" grade levels—who met together during daily division or advisory periods. It turned out that *how* each school dealt with these special groups sent strong messages to students about their status in the school and their "place" in the academic community.

Transitional Advisory at Devon High. Devon put failing students in a "transitional advisory" upon their return to school in the fall if they had not earned sufficient credits to be promoted to the next grade. Students then had 3 extra months to earn the credits that would promote them into the next grade level, at which point they could advance to a regular advisory with their original cohort. If students did not earn enough credits in the fall to be promoted, they would join a regular advisory at the lower grade level. Devon's principal Dr. Antonia explained the logic of this transitional advisory:

> The premise is that students would always be encouraged to continue improving. So you have [credit-deficient students] for whom the concept of getting back in my right grade is really big. . . . They'll have an advisor . . . and somewhere between 7 and 12 to a group, who either don't have the credits, or they don't have the overall percentage [to be promoted], or they're really close in both. The goal of this advisory is exactly what they think it is: to get you into the grade that you just didn't pass [into] with your classmates.

Dr. Antonia assigned Ms. Randolph, the assistant principal, to be the advisor for the transitional advisory between freshman and sophomore years. Alisha appreciated that Ms. Randolph "made us work on our old stuff, and go talk to the teachers." Latrice concurred: "She made us do our work. And that's the assistant principal, too. If you ain't doing your work in her class, then I don't know what to tell you." Latrice concluded that "it was good" she had been assigned to Ms. Randolph "because I did make up a lot of work in her advisory." Though they were in between grade levels, students felt camaraderie with classmates in their transitional advisory and felt like the school's administrators had confidence in them and were helping them succeed.

Demote Division at Alexander High. Maxwell and Alexander also had designated divisions for students who were in between grade levels, but they used a more unfortunate term that was common across the district for these transitional advisories. Chicago students who failed to be promoted were considered instead to be *demoted*, and they were clustered together in "demote divisions." Students within these divisions were commonly referred to as "demotes."

Berger and Luckmann (1966) referred to the "coercive effects" of language in constructing social reality; I wondered about the meaning conveyed to students by their assignment to the demote division, and the effects this language may have had on students' academic self-concept. Dr. Antonia, the principal at Devon, alluded to the symbolic function of demote divisions in regular district high schools where she had previously worked: "They put all the kids who failed the grade in one [demote division]. It was not designed to accelerate their promotion to the right grade. It was to isolate them from having a negative influence on the rest of the class. There was this assumption that if you had failed the grade, you were a loser . . . and it was just inherently, like, derisive and bad." To further the unfortunate symbolism, rather than assigning a highly visible administrator as the advisor, as was the case at Devon, Alexander filled the role with a poorly performing teacher who was subsequently dismissed from the school, followed by a long-term substitute teacher. Principal Jenkins acknowledged the staffing situation was "really unfortunate" insofar as the "temporary teacher in there hasn't really invested as much in trying to get [students] to see that they need to get out."

Principal Jenkins recalled that when Alexander High first opened, the faculty was philosophically opposed to demote divisions. But as students began falling further off-track in earning credits, "I felt like it was giving them a false sense of their status" to be promoted to a regular division in the next grade level with their peers. "Even though the demote division could be more proactive for making sure the students are getting back on track, I still feel like at least the students know where they stand and the parents know."

Faculty and administrators at Alexander were struggling to build a college-going culture in a racially and economically segregated community that had some of the lowest high school graduation rates in the city and very little college-going experience. Although Principal Jenkins realized that "a lot of the students were a little offended" by placement in the demote division, "at the same time, we're not going to have you living in a fantasy world, in a dream world as if you're going to graduate in 4 years if you continue down this path. So it doesn't serve as much of a purpose to the way I guess in the progressive manner you would want it to. But I think it serves the purpose of putting people on notice that, 'You are off-track to graduate.'"

Kendra was reassigned to the demote division at Alexander in spring semester in response to her failing grades in the first half of sophomore year. Once the school had taken the step of concentrating its most academically vulnerable students in one place, what did it do with them? I asked Kendra about academic supports available to her during demote division that might increase her likelihood of success. "We don't do nothing. We don't do nothing. We just sit there, talk, listen to music. Half the time don't nobody be in there, everybody be walking the halls. We don't do nothing." I asked Kendra if she thought it would be better if everyone were just returned to a regular division. "Yeah, 'cause in a regular division, they make you do work, they make you do your homework and stuff. We don't do none of that."

Monique had very similar criticisms of demote division. She noted that division met "once a day. Sometimes it's only 10 minutes, but on full days [once a week] it's like 90 minutes." I asked what happened in division in those long periods. "Well, in this division," Monique replied, "we don't do nothing." Shana had one word for what she saw as the purpose of demote division at Alexander: "Punishment." She said it was probably effective because it made her not want to be there.

Demote Division at Maxwell High. Like Alexander, Maxwell utilized the common structure in the Chicago Public Schools of demote divisions for failing students. Because the school was so much larger than Alexander or Devon and a larger percentage of students had course failures, Maxwell had multiple demote divisions at each grade level. At the time of the Study 1 interviews, Dawson, Sonia, and Rodney were all in a sophomore demote division. Dawson said he was put there because he still "needed to catch up with the sophomores" in his credit accumulation, but he described it as "like a regular division" that offered no particular supports. Rodney offered a more detailed description: "It's just a regular division. It's just different because, like, some of the students don't come to class, or school. It's like once they found out they're demote, they just give up. But I be striving for the best." I asked if students in the demote division got any extra support to help them improve their academic performance. He said, "Not really, we just go in there, get our attendance, sit around, talk."

Sonia seemed to be the Maxwell student most affected by her placement in a demote division. When describing her failure in American Lit, she told me, "I sat at the back of the classroom at the beginning of the year, 'cause . . . I don't even know why. . . . I felt like I didn't belong in there, so I just sat in the back." When I asked her why she felt like she didn't belong, she said,

"Um . . . I don't know. It's a class full of sophomores. . . . I'm a demote . . . so . . . I sat in the back." Later, she explained why she was hesitant to seek help from adults at Maxwell:

> I don't know. Our counselor barely even comes to our [division]. Came once. . . . It just seem like, to me, the school don't really care about the demotes. Like you see the [regular sophomore] divisions, they counselors in and out of there all the time in they divisions, talking to them about what they need to do to pass, and how they need to be learning, and all this other stuff, but we see our counselor [only] once.

She noted that they must be "paying attention 'cause they put us in the [demote] division, but, like, after that, there's no hope for the demotes."

ACADEMIC, MOTIVATIONAL, AND DEVELOPMENTAL DIMENSIONS OF REMEDIATION AND RECOVERY

All three schools offered structured programs for remediation and credit recovery and had dedicated advisories or divisions for students who were in between grades. From their comments above, we can see that students actively participated in Devon's transitional advisory and used it as another opportunity to meet outcomes and recover credits. Maxwell students showed up in their demote division and then sat around. Students at Alexander seemed to place no value on demote division and wanted to avoid it altogether. As Kendra told me, "I don't even need to be in there. I just go in, sign my name, and leave right back out."

All three schools were deeply concerned about students who were "off-track" due to course failures. They actively pushed students to follow the paths laid out for them for remediation and recovery, whether attending academic workshop and summer school at Devon High or attending tutoring, night school, or summer school for students at Maxwell and Alexander. But, as with advisories, there were significant differences in students' participation in the various remediation and recovery programs these schools offered.

Devon students said they participated in academic workshop and Saturday school because they believed it would help them succeed in their classes. Academic workshops allowed them to complete work they had been unable to complete in class or at home. Sharday explained that academic workshop provided "more one-on-one time. It's like the instructions is clearer, and it's less people. So you get time to work, think, turn it in. It's just that simple." Likewise, Diamond said, "It's a one-on-one thing. You just get, like, time with the teacher. . . . No distractions." Brittany said she completed more work in academic workshop "'cause sometimes it's only you there where it's not so loud, so you get the work done like that. There are no distractions." She described an academic workshop she had attended that week staffed by volunteer adult tutors in addition to math teachers:

> Sometime they have math specialists up there, in the math lab, and you work on your math and get it all correct, and [the teacher will change the *Not Yet* rating], so that's one outcome you don't have to worry about. [The math specialists] explain it to you the best way they know how. Like integers, positive and negative numbers, when I first starting doing it I just put anything on the paper. But academic workshop they actually helped me, sit there and help me.

Devon students repeatedly noted that characteristics of academic workshop and Saturday school that facilitated their success were the availability of one-on-one help, the smaller number of students relative to a regular classroom, and the ability to focus without distraction. As a result, Devon students got the academic help they needed.

Interestingly, the features of academic workshop that Devon students reported as being most effective were strikingly similar to the features Alexander students said they liked about night school. Sharday explained why it was easier to learn history and geometry at night school than it was in her regular classrooms at Devon:

> Night school's fun to me. . . . I have more help. . . . I do a lot of work in there, but I get it done. I get it done. He'll either bring like two teachers in [or] like we'll work in groups and we'll just help each other out with whatever we need help. Because that's what I told my momma, I think like I can work [better] in a small group. I cannot work with a big class. Because I get off-track. Like, I can't concentrate on the subject. With people dropping out [of the night school class], it's only five of us [left].

Although it is concerning that so many kids were dropping out of night school, the resulting small class size made it easier for Sharday to concentrate. Monique expressed similar sentiments, saying it was easier to learn algebra in her night class, where the teacher "broke it down, every step, in every way she knew how."

Individualized help, fewer distractions, and a smaller scale were the features that most effectively supported students' achievement in both night school and academic workshop. These features were built into Devon High School's regular operating structure, whereas Alexander students needed to go outside the regular school setting (i.e., to night school) to benefit from them. From the limited information I had on Maxwell's remediation programs, it seemed that students there felt like they did not have enough access to teachers outside of the classroom to get the help they needed.

Developmentally, Devon's academic workshop and transitional advisory encouraged students to be in regular communication with their teachers about their academic performance. Though teachers complained about student procrastination, over time Devon students learned to persist until they met their academic goals. In their daily advisories they learned to organize their work for the week, make plans for the *Not Yets* they would address, and track their ongoing progress. In contrast, I saw no evidence at either Maxwell or Alexander that students got any organized help in developing the kinds of academic habits that would promote their success. Instead, the main message seemed to be that they had done something wrong by failing, and to do better they needed to "strive more."

From a motivational perspective, students' varying levels of participation in school remediation and recovery programs indicate that these programs had varying levels of motivational "pull." Students showed up to academic workshops that connected effort to success, and avoided tutoring programs that felt like a waste of time. As shown in Chapter 3, students who feel a sense of belonging in their academic community demonstrate a much higher level of commitment to academic work and are more likely to keep trying when the work gets hard. The messages schools send to students about their academic status and the *meaning* of that status have strong psychological implications for students' sense of belonging. At Devon, students in transitional advisory saw themselves as being in transition to something better, supported by people who acknowledged them as valued members of a learning community. At Alexander and Maxwell, students labeled as "demotes" saw themselves as being singled out for punishment or flagged as failures. Demote division attenuated their connection to school and made them question their belonging in the academic world.

HOW REMEDIATION AND RECOVERY PROGRAMS AFFECTED STUDENTS' SUCCESS

What became clear to me in conversations with Maxwell and Alexander students was that the recommended paths to credit recovery in those schools were totally unrealistic. Even the most well-prepared, well-supported, and already successful students would have a grueling time sustaining the pace of coursework described by Monique, Kendra, Shana, Dawson, Rodney, and Sonia in their credit recovery plans. In the absence of effective learning strategies, strong adult support, or attitudes and beliefs that bolster success, how would struggling students be able to navigate the path laid out for them and succeed in night school and summer school on top of regular school? The only guidance these kids got were admonitions to strive harder—and indeed, *harder* was the operative word.

I did not have final transcript data for Maxwell students, so I don't know what happened to them after spring semester of their second year of school. However, I do know what happened for the three students at Alexander. Although teachers and administrators had their eye on the ball and acted quickly to enroll credit-deficient students in night school, this recovery strategy had limited effect.

In spring of her second year, Shana had been juggling two night school classes that met 4 nights a week, but this required a substantial time commitment and took a significant toll on her ability to succeed in her regular daytime coursework. She did pass one night class, but she failed three more regular classes that spring. Shana earned a total of 2.5 credits (and a D average) for the semester. She did not attend summer school that year, but in her third and fourth years Shana made up several classes in night school and summer school. Against the odds, Shana got back on track to graduate with her class.

As Monique and Kendra neared the end of their second year of high school, both girls grew increasingly discouraged about their possibilities for success. Kendra failed all but one of her regular classes in spring (she passed Ms. Orozco's class with a D) and didn't even attempt to take any credit recovery classes. At the end of her second year of high school, she was only a half-credit closer to graduation than she had been at the end of freshman year, but seven or eight credits further behind her peers. Even before she got her semester report card, Kendra was looking at a credit recovery plan that included summer school every year, plus numerous night courses, on top of a full load of regular school. Unfortunately, Kendra ended up being barred from summer school that year due to an extended suspension from a fight on the last day of school in June. In her third year, she failed all but one class in fall semester. She transferred to an alternative school in the middle of spring semester, but was officially classified as a dropout.

Monique also had a difficult spring. She tried taking algebra at night school, but she didn't finish the course. By the end of spring semester, Monique failed all her regular classes and earned no night school credits. She was no closer to graduation than she had been at the start of the semester. She enrolled in summer school but was dropped for excessive absences. In her third year of school, she failed all but one class. Monique only attended 1 day of her fourth year of school, and was officially classified as a dropout.

In spring of her sophomore year, Monique told me she thought Alexander High School should provide more academic support, but she also faulted students for giving up. I asked her thoughts on why students gave up on school. "I think because if I keep trying and trying, and I can't, and it won't do nothing for me and I'm still trying, I'm still just struggling. I think that's probably why kids give up. 'Cause they tried" and it didn't matter.

The three Alexander students lost a combined total of 19 credits over 2 years due to failed courses. Though all three participated in structured opportunities for credit recovery (each took at least one night school or summer school class), their efforts over 2 years yielded only one total recovered credit among the three students. This represented a recovery rate of only 5%. Shana may have been better off to focus on her regular classes instead of being distracted by the demands of night school, a thought that no doubt crossed her mind when she ended the semester more credit-deficient (relative to her entering cohort) than she began it. In short, it appears that school and classroom policies and practices at Alexander and the structured opportunities the school offered for credit recovery actually impeded students' success in classes while doing little to help them recover lost credits. My reading of this is not that these kids weren't trying hard enough or wanting it enough. Rather, high school was structured in such a way that once they started failing, their continued failure was almost inevitable.

Three students at Devon—Alisha, Latrice, and Sharday—had roughly equivalent credit histories to the three Alexander students at the start of Study 2: They had failed some 9th-grade classes but had been promoted to taking mostly 10th-grade classes. Combined, these three Devon students lost a total of 25.5 credits over their first 2 years of high school due to failed (*Not Yet*) courses, a much higher rate of failure than for the students at Alexander. They attended summer school and went to academic workshops throughout the school year to remediate their performance in current classes and to recover lost credits from past classes. Through participation in these structured opportunities, over their freshman and sophomore years they were collectively able to recover 12.5 credits, or 49% of the credits they had lost to failure. This is in sharp contrast to the 5% recovery rate at Alexander.

Devon students Diamond and Brittany had the two worst academic records of the eight students in Study 2. They had done so poorly in the first year of high school that their teachers recommended that both students retake all 9th-grade classes so they would have daily structured support for learning. Diamond and Brittany also participated in academic workshop and Saturday school over and above their retaking of freshman courses. Although both students spoke enthusiastically in interviews about the school and the alternative grading system, their beliefs that "success is possible" did not translate into passing classes. Diamond did improve her performance significantly in the second year of high school and was on the cusp of advancement to 10th grade when she moved out of state in the summer, a few months after our interviews. Brittany continued to struggle and failed most of her classes for the second time. After a second year of course failure, Brittany's parents moved her out of Devon High School and into a vocational training program. It is noteworthy, however, that both students consistently expressed positive feelings about the school, their teachers, and their chances for success.

Meanwhile, Alisha passed two classes during her second year at Devon and managed to get credit for an additional three classes in summer school. She earned 5 credits in her sophomore year, for 10 credits total. She was able to advance to 11th-grade coursework in all subjects except math. Alisha continued to struggle academically, but she was on track to graduate in June 2010.

Sharday also earned only two credits in her second year at Devon, but over the summer she was able to recover credits in four additional classes. By September, she had earned 6.5 credits for the previous year, for a credit total of 11.5 at the start of junior year. She was on the cusp (67% and 69% respectively) of earning an additional 1.5 credits for two other courses. Sharday was also on track to graduate, enrolled in all 11th-grade courses, and excited about school.

Latrice earned 3.5 credits in her second year and passed one additional course in summer school, giving her a total of 12.5 credits toward graduation. She, too, was on the verge of receiving credit in two additional classes (worth 1.5 credits), meeting 67% of the outcomes in each, working toward the 70% passing threshold. Latrice was enrolled in all 11th-grade classes and looking forward to graduating in June 2010.

STRUCTURING FAILURE

In studying American schooling and social inequality, Bowles and Gintis (1976) came to this sobering conclusion: "Frequent failures play an important role in gradually bringing a student's aspirations in line with his or her probable career opportunities. By the time most students terminate schooling, they have been put down enough to convince them of their inability to succeed at the next highest level" (p. 106). Students who experience continual defeat in their high school classrooms eventually respond by lowering their aspirations and reconciling themselves to the truncated opportunities that await them.

Indeed, over time, failing students in Alexander and Maxwell high schools began to downgrade their expectations for the future, to resign themselves to a lesser fate. Many began defining "success" quite loosely as not failing any additional classes. After a string of Fs in sophomore math, Shana concluded,

"It's not looking good. I'm trying to get to a D or something." When I asked Monique what chances she gave herself for graduating in 2 years with her class, she answered immediately, "A hundred percent." After a moment's thought, she said, "But the way my grades looking now . . . [more] like ten." When Sonia looked at what she would need to do to retrieve her lost credits (2 or 3 years of night school and summer school), she brought up another possibility. "I don't know, I was thinking about my junior year, going to another school, [an] alternative school to make up my credits, and then coming back senior year to graduate with my class," although she admitted, "my dad said he didn't want me to do that." Sonia didn't know how alternative school worked, but "I know . . . that it's easier." She had all but given up on making it through regular high school.

Devon students, in contrast, seemed to maintain a very positive sense of their potential for academic success, even when the evidence was overwhelmingly to the contrary, as was the case with Brittany and Diamond. Principal Dr. Antonia listed the many ways Devon students came into school with socioeconomic disadvantages that had a negative impact on their academic performance. But given all of that, she said,

> You still want everybody to learn and achieve at the highest level. Some kids are going to take more time. They have not learned how to learn in a rapid and efficient way. Their learning processes are very labored. Their efficiencies are very limited. And so allowing for that is also really important. Rather than stigmatizing that in a way that says, "You're stupid. You're slow. You're special ed. You're a loser," you say, "Well, that's okay. You need to come on Thursday afternoon. You need to come on Saturday. No, you still don't get it. You have to come in this summer."

Dr. Antonia saw the school's alternative structures, policies, and practices as essential tools in promoting social justice rather than reinforcing the ideology of stratification. She did not want her students to come to terms with personal failure as their lot in life. She continued:

> That's more of the tension I face. I want to encourage [students] to be the best they can be, to really strive for the most, but then [to also] understand that society is not really opening a lot of doors. . . . You want them to be aware that for equity and social justice to be achieved, there has to be some structural and social changes—which they should feel justified in demanding—because they're no longer believing, "I really am just a loser who might as well have just dropped out. . . . Opportunities aren't there [for me], because opportunities are really only offered

to good people, and I'm not one of them." And so to me, that's really the challenge in public schools. How do you create [the] expectation that every child coming up is one of the good people, and that they all deserve real opportunities?

She and her faculty worked every day to create a school that could construct that reality for their students.

DOING THE SAME THING AND EXPECTING DIFFERENT RESULTS

I have argued that failure has a long history in American secondary schools, serving an important selection and stratification function. Time-based learning opportunities, course credits, points, and letter grades, these are all aspects of American high schools designed to stratify student achievement, to determine who is best and who is not. The notion that learning is an individual accomplishment is reinforced through repeated cycles of assessment and grading; we put great stock in scores, grades, points, percents, and all the myriad ways we have of calculating how students stack up against one another.

Our entire system of secondary instruction and assessment rests on a series of fundamental beliefs. First and foremost, we believe that points and grades and such are accurate measures of student achievement. They tell us who truly *is* better or smarter or more skillful or more knowledgeable—and who is not. We believe that 81% is exactly that much better than 79%, and so deserves a different letter as we enter grades in our record books. And though we know that the world is full of disparities that affect our students outside of school, we strive to make sure that everything we do *inside* of school is fair and objective. We go out of our way to level the playing field. Recognizing that students have family responsibilities that prevent them from doing homework, we give extra weight to in-class assignments. Knowing that poor health or lack of transportation can interfere with student attendance, we devise ways to bring students up to speed when they return to school and give extra time to submit missed assignments. Acknowledging that students fail even amid these supports, we immediately enroll them in night school or summer school to recover their credits. Though the world is not fair, we believe that everyone in our classrooms has a roughly equal shot at success, or at least as equal as we can make possible.

As teachers and administrators, we also know that we work incredibly hard, and that we care about the well-being of the young people who come into our classrooms every day. We want to feel successful and competent as professionals, and we want students to feel successful and competent in our classes and in their lives outside of school. *This is why we became educators.* But sometimes it can seem like we are putting in a disproportionate share of effort into the success of students who do not succeed, and we get worn down by their failure. We are also stuck in a system that requires that we grade students, and we can only give them the grades they earn. Even if we are convinced that failure is "bad" and doesn't serve our students well, that doesn't mean we can let them pass if their work doesn't warrant it. To do so would be unfair to everybody else, to the ones who are doing what we asked of them.

So we do the best we can within the constraints of this traditional system, and students continue to fail at alarming rates. Sometimes we blame the system that constrains us, sometimes we blame our school leaders or district or state administrators or the policies they create, sometimes we blame the kids and their families. And we continue to do what teachers have done for the past hundred-plus years: We teach, we support, we assess, we record the grades, and we move on to the next unit.

They say that lunacy is doing the same thing over and over again and expecting different results. If we continue to funnel students through the same structures, policies, and practices that currently constitute the American public high school, we most assuredly will continue to get the same results. Failure and dropout are by-products of this process *by design.*

Medical professionals working for systematic healthcare improvement—efforts that have resulted in significantly fewer patient deaths in U.S. hospitals—make this point more directly. As Dartmouth professor of pediatrics Paul Batalden is fond of saying, "Every system is perfectly designed to get the results it gets." High schools produce student failure not because something has gone awry, but rather because everything is working perfectly. We may have changed our goals for high schools over the past hundred years, and teachers may have the very best intentions to help students succeed, but we won't get different results *if we do not change the system itself.*

EIGHT

Teacher Practices That Support Student Effort

Everybody wants to succeed. The students at Maxwell, Alexander, and Devon High Schools all cared about school, wanted to do well in their classes, and placed great value on earning a diploma. They entered 9th grade with high hopes and expectations for success. When they began to fail, they talked about the importance of putting in more effort, trying harder. They knew intuitively—and the adults around them reinforced the idea—that they weren't going to succeed in school if they didn't work hard. But what moves students from an abstract commitment to schooling to actually putting in the hard work required to succeed?

Chapter 3 reviewed four academic mindsets that are strongly associated with academic perseverance and good grades: "I belong in this academic community," "I can succeed at this," "My ability and competence grow with my efforts," and "This work has value for me." Students who believe any of these statements are more likely to invest effort in learning and to persist in the face of adversity. The psychological research paints a clear picture: When students care about what they are learning, see a clear path to developing valued knowledge and skills, envision themselves on that path, believe their efforts will pay off, and trust they will be supported when they need it, they are much more likely to work hard to learn. We saw in Chapters 6 and 7 how grading policies and structured programs for remediation and credit recovery affected students' beliefs that their ability and competence would grow with effort, their expectations for success in school, and their sense of belonging in their classroom communities.

By the time I spoke with the students featured in these pages, three semesters of failing grades gave them reason to question the likelihood of their own academic success and belonging in school. Even when students expressed the belief that success was possible, they did not feel it to be equally possible in all their courses. Academic achievement, it seemed, was determined as much by the classroom as by the student. So what contributed to the possibility of academic success?

In Study 2, I asked each student to tell me about a current class in which she was feeling *most* competent and successful, as well as a current class in which she was feeling the *least* competent and successful. I observed all of both kinds of classes and interviewed all of those teachers. I also reviewed interview transcripts from Study 1 for students' descriptions of classes in which they were successful and those in which they were not. Together, their comments illuminate conditions under which students will work to learn and strongly suggest that teachers have great power over student motivation and effort. Across all three schools, there was remarkable similarity in students' descriptions of the conditions that support success.

"I CAN SUCCEED AT THIS"

Students felt more competent and successful when teachers demonstrated genuine care for their well-being and provided support and encouragement to ensure that they learned. Monique pointed out that a significant level of care was not always possible in high school: "In elementary school, teachers—they take more pain—well, I don't want to say pain, but they take more time with one student, and in high school, you know, there's so many students that they can't do that." Yet students appreciated when teachers asked about them and showed an interest in what was going on in their lives. Kendra described her World Studies teacher as a "good teacher" because "when I be having problems I talk to her. . . . She help me out. She be there for me." Likewise, Monique appreciated that her division teacher noticed when she got a failing grade in one class. "[She] would ask why I was like getting—why did I have that F. And I explained to her and she like, 'Well, you'll do better next marking period.' She asked me—she be like, 'If you need any help . . . you know the people that's around here can help you.'"

Conversely, when teachers did *not* show care and concern, students felt less motivated to put in effort. I asked Monique whether her teachers said anything when she missed school. "No," she told me. "None of them." She went on to explain:

> Some teachers be like, "I don't care. I got mine, like whether you get it or not, I'm still gonna get paid." So some of them, it's just about the money. . . . You're like, okay, if you just wanted the money—come on, you're teaching! It's supposed to come from the heart. It's something that you should want to do, not just—hmm.

Monique shook her head in dismay.

Beyond demonstrating care for their well-being, students pointed to teachers who actively supported their efforts to learn. Brittany directly attributed feeling "competent and successful" in one class to her teacher's support. After having failed the same class with a different teacher the year before, Brittany noted that "this year, I didn't have to ask for help, she'd just come over and help me."

Several students at Devon identified Ms. Michael's humanities class as the place where they felt most competent and successful. They gave numerous examples of the ways their teacher helped them learn. Diamond said Ms. Michael encouraged her when she was confused. She offered a sample of a typical conversation: "When she teach, everybody gets something out of it. If I don't get nothing, I'm like, 'Ms. Michael, can you come over here and help me out on this?' And she'll say, 'Yeah, all you got to do is just write this down, see. . . .' 'You mean like this?' 'Yeah, you got it! See? All you need is a little help. You got it!'" Diamond was excited about an essay introduction she had written in Ms. Michael's class for which she got very positive feedback from her teacher. "She was like, 'That was good! That's eye-catching! You know it would catch your eye, make the reader want to read more.' And I'm like, okay! I'm really doing it! I'm doing good!"

Latrice gave a similar account of Ms. Michael's encouragement. "She's, like, really confident in us. Not saying all our teachers not, but she explain it. World War II and the Holocaust. We have conversations on it. Then we take tests on it. If we get it wrong, then she be like, 'Nah, this is what it is, this is what it is. You study it, come back and retake it.' So it's made me like, ever since I been in [her class], I've never failed in that."

In comparison, Latrice thought some teachers were condescending when students asked questions. Taking on a patronizing tone, she mimicked, "Uh, no, sweetheart, that's wrong." Ms. Michael, on the other hand, "She'll be like, no, this is such and such, such and such. Then she'll break down the answer, then we have a discussion about it." The big difference, Latrice said, was "mainly she won't make us feel stupid about something." As a result of her teacher's support, Latrice said she worked harder in Ms. Michael's class than she did in other classes.

Beyond being friendly and encouraging, Ms. Michael employed specific practices that helped students feel supported. Diamond said Ms. Michael routinely sent out emails to individual students, "like if we missing work or we need help on something, or if we failing something we don't know we failing, she email us. She let us know that we can come to her for anything." When assigning a large project, Ms. Michael gave students a packet with clear directions and examples for each part of the assignment and references for more resources. Diamond said that, as a result, she felt like she knew what she was expected to do.

At Alexander High School, Monique identified her music class as the place she felt most competent and successful. She said she worked hard in that class and learned a lot, even when she did not feel like doing work.

When I asked her what her music teacher did that made it easier to learn, she said, "This is what Ms. Canter told us. She was like, you know, she had to teach people how to sing. She said she had prayed to God to send her a class that [already] know how to sing and she wouldn't have to do all that work." The teacher made her class feel as though they were the answer to her prayers. "So," Monique concluded, "it's pretty easy" to feel competent in her class.

Diamond said her Spanish teacher helped her feel successful in a difficult class. "I was just thinking, like, okay, I'm *never* gonna get Spanish," when her teacher approached and told her, "You're doing so good in my class." The teacher's encouragement made her feel more committed to working hard. "I was actually paying attention, and listening to what she was saying, so that I could get it." Though missing work was the cause of her failure in most other classes, she said in Spanish "I turned in my work . . . [and] I'm going to keep doing it."

Contrast this with Sharday's description of a class in which she was *not* feeling competent and successful. In science, "I do all this work for her class, and she still saying I don't do enough. So you feel like . . . you just gonna focus on some other class instead." I asked her what was likely to happen in science at the end of the year. "I'll probably fail," she answered with a tone of resignation. "I don't want to fail it, though." Similarly, Kendra spoke of a teacher who made it hard to feel motivated in a class she was failing. "She have a bad attitude. She holler at us. She want us to respect her, but she don't respect us. She be hollering. She had a real, real, real bad attitude."

Monique expressed appreciation for teachers that take the "time and pains" to explain things so that students can understand. A good teacher, when "you don't understand something, they don't act like they get frustrated 'cause you don't understand it. They try to break it down, each step and each word and try to" make sure you are learning. Alisha said that when teachers "explain good," it makes her work harder. "'Cause if I get it, then I do all my work. But if I don't get it, I'm gonna sit there and don't know what to do."

In a supportive classroom, Diamond said she felt more independent. "We have little debates in the classroom, and I always lead a group," she told me excitedly. The experience of leading groups in class "shows me that I [can be] independent. Like I can do it and I don't need nobody else to be behind me or be in front of me. I can do it myself."

Kendra said that for her, support came in the form of making sure she was not falling further behind when she missed classes. "Like if I'm suspended, when I come back Ms. Orozco get my makeup work. Other teachers, I be having to go to them and ask them, a couple of days [of asking], or if I forget about it and I'm not asking them, they just don't say nothing and mark it as zero and I end up getting a F. But she keep calling me and telling me, I'm missing this, I'm missing that."

Shana also identified Ms. Orozco's class as the place she felt most competent and successful. "I guess 'cause I'm comfortable in there. She, you know, she talk to us more. She's like a honest person. Like, if she feel that you need help, she'll tell you. She not like the other teachers, like 'You need to do this' and all that type of stuff. She'll just tell you, but in a nice way. So, like, she's a concerning teacher. She concerned about her students." Shana said the difference between classes in which she did well and classes in which she struggled "depends on how the teachers teach." She thought that some teachers made it feel easy to learn. "But then it's like, some other class, you be like . . . you just stuck. Ms. Orozco makes it easy. . . . She make it better for us to understand."

Alisha had similar comments about her 9th-grade math teacher, saying, "She talked the way I learn." Though students' feelings of confidence were sometimes subject-specific—for example, a student may generally have more positive feelings about English than about science—often students talked about serious differences within the same subject area from one teacher to another. Alisha's experience in 9th-grade math seemed to be one of effortlessness or "flow" (Csikszentmihalyi, 1990). "Like if she was teaching us stuff, I give it back right then and there. I don't know how, but I just did." In contrast, Alisha really struggled with her sophomore math teacher. "I don't get nothing she be talking about. I don't know what's going on."

Latrice had a similar experience. She felt as though her sophomore math teacher was "always arguing with her students every day. She like nitpicks on people." Latrice said, "I could just be sitting there, laying my head down waiting for her to explain," when the teacher will reprimand her: "Get up. I'm not playing freshman baby games today." Instead of embracing the kinds of activities that her students enjoyed (here Latrice referenced the debates, movie clips, and discussions in Ms. Michael's classroom), she said the math teacher dismissed those as more "baby games." "She like, 'Well, this is what it gonna be like in the real world.'" Latrice said the math teacher was always threatening that students would have to go to summer school if they did not work harder, which she interpreted as the teacher shifting all the responsibility for learning onto the students, like "I got mine, you need to get yours." "I feel like I understand you got your own," Latrice told me. "You wouldn't be teaching me if you don't. [But] you know, you need to let me get mine." The negative impact of a teacher was just as profound as the potential positive impacts. Latrice said she had passed 92% of her math outcomes in freshman year and felt confident in her math ability, but in her second year she was failing. "I actually like math. I wanted to major in mathematics. She just made me change my whole mind."

"THIS WORK HAS VALUE FOR ME"

Students felt more competent and successful when classroom activities were interesting and able to hold their attention or when students felt they were developing useful knowledge and skills. Across all three schools, students articulated a clear connection between interest, focus, and learning. As Diamond put it, when classes are "boring, then you don't focus, you're not focusing no more." For her part, Brittany said she wanted teachers to teach in a way that "make kids actually want to learn and not just go in one ear and out the other." For her, that happened when teachers related schoolwork "to real life, what's happening with kids every day in everyday life." She gave the example of her science class where a day-long river trip was the centerpiece of a larger unit of study. Students conducted experiments, applied what they were learning in a real context, and later presented their results to a volunteer panel of judges. "I like the river trip," Brittany said with enthusiasm. Interestingly, that science class was the only core high school course Brittany ever passed.

Students generally preferred hands-on activities to teacher lectures. At Alexander, several students pointed to a particular history classroom in which they did *not* feel "competent and successful." They attributed this in part to their teacher's style of instruction. Although some students acknowledged that he was "a good teacher," still Shana told me, "most of the time you're just kind of sitting there and he's talking. . . . And I just nod off and go to sleep." She thought her previous year's history class was "more funner." That class got to go to the computer lab, do projects, and play simulation games. "You know, you do like the games with the work. You get to act out stuff. It was fun." Shana concluded, "I guess it depends on how teachers teach."

Students' self-perceptions also seemed to change depending on the classroom and how interested they were in what they were learning. Courtney failed several of her classes because, she told me, "I'm lazy." Later, she described her art and photography classes, things she said she was "good at." She told me, "When you take pictures it's just like, everything else goes away. You're just focusing on that one thing to make it perfect. And like, for art, you're just expressing yourself and who you are, and you just don't let anyone bother you." I asked if she was lazy in art and photography. "Uh, no," she replied, rather incredulously.

Latrice had been talking for some time about how interesting it was to learn about World War II in humanities class. She told me she never liked social studies in elementary school. I asked why she was so interested in learning history now. "It's like maybe it was the learning, the different ways of being taught," she told me. "'Cause my teacher in elementary school was just like so dead. And if you dead, the students gonna be dead." In contrast, she found the study of Hiroshima to be "challenging," which added to her interest. "It's like no one wants to sit up there and do boring work. I don't like doing stuff that I already did. I like stuff that's interesting, that like, gets you thinking."

THE MOTIVATIONAL DIMENSION OF STUDENT ACHIEVEMENT

Human beings, regardless of age, do their best work under certain sets of conditions. When they believe they can succeed, when they feel they belong and that their work will contribute to a larger community, when they see their efforts rewarded with the improvement or advancement they are seeking, and when the work itself is meaningful to them or will get them someplace they want to go—under these conditions human beings will put forth unlimited effort toward a goal. High school students are no different. Our 14 students put forth effort to learn when they saw a clear path to success, had teachers who cared about them and made them feel like valued members of the classroom community, experienced a direct connection between their work and their improving grades or accumulating credits, and found the work fun or interesting or relevant.

Individual teachers could create these conditions within their classrooms to a great extent, but larger school structures either reinforced these favorable conditions or they undercut them. It was hard for students to believe that their ability and competence grew with their effort, for example, if school policies imposed significant penalties for late work such that effort stopped paying dividends once a student fell behind. Nonetheless, within individual classrooms, teachers who demonstrated concern for the young people in front of them, who took the time to check on their well-being and were attentive to their academic progress, who patiently explained and then re-explained until students understood a lesson, and who worked to make their classrooms active and interesting places, these teachers elicited a level of effort and commitment from students that didn't happen in other classes. Broadly speaking, these were the classes that the students passed.

Part III

GOING FORWARD

Failure is not fatal, but failure to change might be.

—John Wooden

NINE

Motivation, Capacity, Competence, Opportunity

Redesigning Urban High Schools for Student Success

When people of any age set out to learn a new skill or acquire knowledge that challenges them, they seldom succeed on their first try. As they learn, they are likely to get confused, make mistakes, hit dead ends, flounder, and fail. The higher we aspire and the further we venture into unfamiliar terrain, the more likely we are to mess up and get it wrong. *This is how people learn!* Schools—of all places—should be enthusiastically celebrating failure and fostering processes to help students (and adults) learn from it. Instead, we treat student failure as an aberration, a personal shortcoming, a shameful affront. And far too often, schools structure academic failure in a way that penalizes and irrevocably harms kids. If we are to have any hope of raising a generation capable of solving the problems of the 21st century, what we desperately need are public high schools that encourage young people to stretch beyond their competence and to feel both determined and confident enough to risk failing, again and again, in pursuit of noble goals.

We do well to remember that academic failure has no inherent meaning in and of itself. We imbue failure with significance by how we construct it, explain it, and respond to it. As the experiences of students in this book have illuminated, how failure is "built" in a given school and how educators intervene in the process of academic failure matter greatly for students' motivation, effort, learning, and long-term outcomes.

In the introductory chapter, I contrasted the structure and purpose of failure in the U.S. Air Force Academy with failure in a local parks department basketball program. As in the Air Force Academy, failure as an instrument of *selection and stratification* has its place, but I hope I have convinced you that high school should not be that place. Failing grades, course failure, credit deficiency, grade retention, and dropout are wholly miseducative as traditionally structured. The current breadth, depth, and consequence of student failure point to a fundamental misalignment between high schools and the adolescents they purport to educate, and whatever is going awry goes particularly so for minority students in urban schools. Rather than supporting young people to realize their enormous potential, our construction of failure in the American high school actively reproduces stark inequality.

We tell kids everyone can succeed by their brains and efforts, but then we selectively support some students in their academic endeavors as we systematically undermine others. Those who enter high school equipped with financial resources and effective strategies for learning, with access to health care and transportation, with expectations of going to college like family members before them, with established academic track records and confidence in their own abilities, with membership in social groups that reinforce their sense of belonging in school, and with awareness of the connection between schoolwork and their own goals or interests—these young people are likely to benefit from high school exactly as it is. They are likely to possess academic mindsets that compel them to work hard and persevere in school. Even when their adolescent behavior or "goofy ways" threaten to derail them, they are surrounded by family, peers, teachers, even strangers who expect them to keep marching forward toward a positive future—a future to which they have come to feel *entitled*. As a result, these young people usually do very well in school. (Ironically, even if they *don't* excel in school, these same sets of advantages help them do well in life *anyway*. But that is another book.)

Conversely, students who come to high school with few resources or learning strategies, without access to health care or transportation, with a middling academic history and uncertainty about their abilities, with a relative lack of skills and no compelling connection to what is happening in their classes, saddled with negative stereotypes about their intellect or their drive, and for whom college is an abstract goal—these students are likely to develop mindsets that work against their efforts. They begin to seriously question their own competence and "place" in intellectual environments. They interpret setbacks as indicative of their lack of ability. They struggle to make themselves focus on coursework that holds no inherent meaning for them. As a result, many cannot sustain the effort required for academic success, and they fail, reaffirming every stereotype the larger society has about them and every doubt they have about themselves. When they try to rally back, following the paths to redemption laid out by their schools and teachers, they instead find themselves slipping further behind as they struggle to raise their grades or earn credits toward graduation. These students are no less deserving, no less intelligent, no less capable, no less earnest, and no less indispensable than the students who do well in school. They are just less advantaged. They are also the ones whose futures are *most* dependent on their success in school.

Through the generosity of 14 students willing to share their personal experiences, I endeavored to illustrate exactly how and why urban school failure happens and—perhaps more important—why it seems to be such a permanent condition as constructed in traditional secondary schools. In Maxwell and Alexander high schools—two schools with top-notch principals and many caring and competent teachers—students who fell behind and failed classes in 9th grade were very unlikely to recover from this early failure. In contrasting their experiences with those of students at Devon High, I hope to have shown that academic failure is daily constructed by structures, policies, and practices enacted by well-intentioned administrators and educators, and that there is absolutely nothing inevitable about the abysmal outcomes we have grown to expect in urban schools. Though pervasive messages about intelligence, ability, meritocracy, and deservingness shape our conception of academic failure in the United States, schools and teachers have the power to reframe or override these messages and create something different. In this last chapter, I offer an alternative vision for public secondary education. This vision is by no means new. For as long as there have been public high schools, educators and reformers have periodically called for many of these same recommendations. Sometimes these initiatives got a little traction, sometimes whole systems moved, but eventually schools and teachers slid back to old ways of doing things. We need to know this going in: High schools are rather impervious to change.

Still, I believe there is cause for hope. We know much more about human motivation and learning than we ever knew before. We have a much clearer idea of conditions that support students' academic efforts and the cognitive, social, and emotional processes involved in developing expertise and building skills. We are expanding our understanding of classroom environments and instructional practices that help kids learn and grow into thoughtful, engaged adults. We can, if we so choose, apply this vast array of knowledge to organizing equitable and excellent high schools.

Many educators are already doing exactly this in urban schools around the country. I am inspired by places like the Expeditionary Learning Schools or the High Tech High network, where kids from a wide range of backgrounds routinely produce incredibly high-quality work. It is amazing what young people can do when they are engaged in personally and socially meaningful projects, given the opportunity to pursue their own questions, and supported by adults with utmost faith in their ability to deliver. Such schools provide existence proof not only that poor kids of color can *achieve*, but that virtually all young people are capable of far more than we might think possible.

I am also encouraged by a growing consensus on the need to transform secondary education, as well as the political will to do so, at least in some quarters. Educators, researchers, policymakers, and philanthropic foundations are shifting to a focus on "deeper learning" that builds student expertise and transferrable knowledge to equip students to engage in the world and address its challenges (e.g., Alliance for Excellent Education, 2011; National Research Council, 2012; William and Flora Hewlett Foundation, 2010). All but a handful of states have adopted the Common Core State Standards, providing a solid set of learning goals and instructional targets for K–12 educators. These common standards are not just about making academic work harder. They represent a strong move away from worksheets, disconnected facts, and status quo instructional methods, instead emphasizing critical thinking, collaborative problem solving, and active learning as the educational due of *all* students.

Further, many schools and districts are finally cutting themselves free from the Carnegie unit, moving to standards-based grading and competency-based learning. For example, superintendents in Connecticut have articulated radical changes to their statewide education system, moving away from "age-based cohorts" and "traditional staffing models" to new "transformative practices" that include progress-based groupings and flexible instructional delivery, where "progress toward graduation [is] measured by authentic learning" rather than seat time (Connecticut Association of Public School Superintendents, 2012). All of this gives me great hope.

The American public high school has provided us with 150 years' worth of lessons in failure. It is probably time we took notes, reassessed our work, and turned a new page. In this last chapter, I describe key components to restructuring public high schools to serve an equity and excellence function. I set this discussion in the context of Common Core State Standards implementation, an educational reform with enormous potential for good or ill.

LEARNING, FAILURE, AND THE COMMON CORE

Educators in the coming decade have a monumental challenge. The widespread adoption of the Common Core State Standards launches us into an era of higher expectations, more rigorous work, more demanding academic content, and an increased emphasis on critical thinking and problem-solving skills. The Common Core will be asking students to engage in work that the majority of students in urban high schools currently don't know how to do. A sure prescription for increasing failure rates is to raise academic expectations without providing the structures and supports that would allow students to meet those higher expectations.

Unfortunately, most urban adolescents attend high schools designed to cull out losers. And we have positioned low-income racial/ethnic minorities as "students most likely to" fail classes and drop out of school. Unless we interrupt this process, the Common Core Standards will simply provide further fodder for the machinations of stratification. All else being equal, teachers will increase academic demands, and more students will fall shorter of the mark. If failure sets them down the path described in these pages, those initial failures could change the entire educational trajectories of new, untold numbers of students. This is the very real risk of substantially more difficult academic standards.

The Common Core State Standards also provide incredible opportunity by declaring that all students deserve an intellectually demanding education. The Common Core rejects the notion that some people are made for lesser things. If we educate every student to the level of knowledge and skill embedded in the Common Core Standards, this will be revolutionary indeed. Whether these new academic standards deepen the stratification that already divides American society or serve as a force for equity and excellence depends on how we address the four dimensions of student achievement. The ultimate impact of the Common Core Standards rests on our answers to these essential questions:

- How do we motivate students to struggle intellectually with very demanding material?
- How do we quickly build students' capacity to do difficult work?
- How do we respond when students fall short?

Perhaps the most important overriding question is this: What would schools need to look like to do all those things reliably well? The remaining pages attempt to briefly sketch out some critical parts of this picture.

SCHOOLS THAT SUPPORT MOTIVATION, BUILD CAPACITY, EXPAND COMPETENCE, AND STRUCTURE OPPORTUNITY

As the experiences of our 14 students have illustrated, school achievement has motivational, developmental, academic, and structural dimensions critically important to an alternative vision for secondary education. Motivationally, students need classrooms and schools that support their natural inclination to learn, encourage them to achieve academic goals, and—if and when they fail—frame that experience in a way that reinforces their pursuit of learning. Developmentally, they need to acquire and practice strategies that will allow them to engage productively with increasingly difficult material. Academically, students need opportunities to build their skills, expand their knowledge, and increase their competence. Structurally, schools should be designed to facilitate the motivational, developmental, and academic needs of students, and to provide struggling students with realistic opportunities to learn from their mistakes, improve their performance, and advance toward graduation. Achieving equity and excellence for the 21st century means redesigning schools to support students' motivation to learn, build their capacity to achieve, expand their knowledge and skills, and structure repeated opportunities for their academic success.

Supporting Students' Motivation to Learn

Humans are naturally inclined to learn. The trick is creating schools that don't kill that inclination, but rather channel it to allow students to reach new heights. Teachers have incredible—often untapped—power over student motivation. How teachers build relationships, structure daily lessons, set and enforce rules, provide feedback and support, and frame academic challenges all have huge implications for student motivation. Motivationally supportive schools and classrooms are characterized by high academic expectations and the conviction that students can reach them, clear connections between academic learning and students' interests and goals, and choice and autonomy in learning activities. They are classroom communities in which students trust adults, receive detailed feedback on their work, and feel a sense of belonging and connection. What they are *not* are places where grades are expected to carry the motivational weight. If teachers believe the only thing making students do their work is the threat of an F or the goal of an A, chances are good that those classrooms are misaligned with students' natural motivation to learn.

One of the primary tasks of adolescence is the development of a healthy identity, a sense of oneself as a competent person with a meaningful place in the world. Failing grades, losing credits, and being held back at year's end while your classmates advance, these experiences all undermine students' sense of personal competence and diminish their agency. Students in my studies felt embarrassed, angry, anxious, and ashamed when they failed. They resolved to try harder, and then they failed again, further deepening their disappointment *in themselves*. Many eventually gave up. What makes dropping out of school doubly tragic is not only that students will likely pay lifelong economic consequences, but that many come to believe they are incompetent, somehow *less than*; they leave high school diminished as they embark on adulthood. Students' sense of their own potential is crushed by repeated failure. Not only does failure interfere with healthy identity development, it also quashes academic motivation. Teachers hope that failing grades will be a "wake-up call" that spurs underperforming students into action. But research has shown repeatedly that adolescents are much more likely to *withdraw* their efforts in response to failure than be encouraged to work harder. Students largely feel "incapable and inadequate" when they fail, promoting "a negative and sometimes devastating effect" on their motivation and self-esteem (Kaplan, Peck, & Kaplan, 1997, p. 331).

Using Counter-Narratives to Support Academic Mindsets. The motivational and identity components of school performance are intertwined with students' academic mindsets—their beliefs about academic work and their own capacity to succeed at it. As described in Chapter 3, students' feelings of self-efficacy, belonging, relevance, and beliefs about the growth potential of their intelligence can have strong effects on how much effort students invest in academic tasks and whether they persevere when they encounter obstacles and challenges.

Unfortunately, there is strong evidence that racial stereotypes, long-standing ideas about intelligence and effort, and a pervasive narrative about minority student underachievement all affect urban adolescents' academic identities and beliefs about themselves as intellectual beings. Schools from coast to coast brandish slogans that "All Kids Can Achieve," but how many educators fully believe that about *all* kids, especially in low-performing urban districts where most students enter high school lacking fundamental knowledge and skills and where only a small subset ever meet grade-level standards? Black and Latino youth have to contend with doubts about whether they belong in academically challenging classes or whether peers or teachers think they are intellectually capable. These troubling thoughts physically diminish students' cognitive capacity for thinking about academic work in the moment and can decrease their motivation and effort in school over the long run.

Claude Steele (2010) makes the argument that it is not that minority students suffer "psychic damage" from stereotypes, but rather that they are interrupted and distracted by them, surrounded by a narrative that is counterproductive to their academic success. Neuroscientists have demonstrated that worries about one's competence take up bandwidth that could otherwise be utilized in cognitive processing (Schmader & Johns, 2003). Experimental studies show that simply reminding students of their minority status prior to an academic task impairs their performance on that task (Good, Aronson, & Inzlicht, 2003; Steele & Aronson, 1995). What must be the effect of unrelenting exposure to a pervasive narrative of personal failure, achievement gaps, and minority student underperformance?

Schools designed for equity and excellence recognize the psychological dimensions of academic experience and create safe spaces for students to learn. They work to secure for students the "freedom to concentrate on academic tasks without constant concern about . . . one's cultural identity" (Gordon & Bridglall, 2006, p. 67). Ironically, African American students in segregated Black schools of the South may have been more likely to experience the kinds of conditions that support academic achievement than they do in most urban schools today. In the pre-civil-rights era, writes Simmons College professor Theresa Perry, "most, if not all, historically black schools and colleges were intentionally organized in opposition to the ideology of black intellectual inferiority. Besides promoting education—an act of insurgency in its own right—they were designed to affirm black humanity, intelligence, and achievement." Teachers in these institutions "intentionally and systematically gave their students a counter-narrative about themselves . . . [and] routinely promoted attitudes, behaviors, and practices that countered the identities of their students as members of an oppressed group" (Perry, 2003, p. B10).

Equitable and excellent schools can take up this banner and actively defuse the negative effects of racial or gender stereotypes and a history of systematic oppression. By reframing larger societal narratives, teachers can provide students with alternative lenses through which to interpret their experience. These counternarratives were clearly necessary under Jim Crow. Helping Black and Latino students to forge social identities as achievers is just as essential today. This can be done by creating school cultures of high academic expectations and larger social purpose, and explicitly including minority students as full participants in that culture of meaningful achievement. You will recall Devon's principal Dr. Antonia talking about helping students develop a critique of existing social structures that allowed them to demand change, while also developing an understanding of themselves as competent people with valuable contributions to make.

The stories we tell act powerfully on our understandings of who we are, of those around us, and of the situations in which we find ourselves. Social psychologists successfully used "narrative interventions" in many of the mindset experiments referred to in Chapter 3. For example, to counteract stereotypes about African American intellectual inferiority or student doubts about belonging, Black and White students entering a predominantly White college were shown videos that depicted academic struggle and self-doubt as something that happened to everybody when they first got to college. The experiment was designed to help Black students reinterpret their sense of profound displacement not as indicative of their being in the wrong institution, but as a normal part of adjusting to college. The African American students who saw that video message ended up earning higher grades, being happier and more engaged in school, and staying in college longer than African American students who saw a different, less targeted message (Steele, 2010; Yeager & Walton, 2011). These kinds of interventions demonstrate that objective features of an educational setting are sometimes less important than our *interpretation of day-to-day experiences* within that setting. The meaning we ascribe to daily interactions "can have great impact on who we think we are and what is possible for us to achieve. "As shown by these interventions," subtle contextual shifts can powerfully change the sense made of daily experiences" (Oyserman, Terry, & Bybee, 2002, p. 315).

To challenge pervasive narratives of academic deficiency, Gloria Ladson-Billings (1994) long ago called for "culturally relevant teaching" that "allows African American students to choose academic excellence yet still identify with African and African American culture" (p. 17). Luis Moll asked educators to seek out the expertise residing within students' homes and families that equips them with skills and knowledge that could be leveraged in classrooms (Moll, Amanti, Neff, & Gonzalez, 1992). Moll and colleagues investigated social and labor histories of Mexican American students' families in rural Arizona, finding a wealth of expertise in farming, construction, mining, and medicine. Once teachers became aware of these rich cultural "funds of knowledge," they figured out how to use family expertise to engage students in traditional classroom subjects (math, history, and so on). Moll's work intentionally shifted the collective narrative about students' families from one of deficits to one of untapped academic assets.

The stories we construct matter. Teachers too often exchange stories with their peers that highlight student deficits or incompetence, perhaps as a way to contend with their own struggles in meeting the many needs of teenagers under their care. Both as a teacher and now as a visitor in high schools all over the country, I hear three familiar narratives from teachers: students who don't care about school, students who lack basic skills necessary for deep intellectual work, and students who have no aspirations to guide them. We (and our students) would do much better if we could reframe these stories of professional difficulty and student inadequacy, instead sharing stories that recognize students' intellectual ability and illuminate a path to help students reach their academic potential. Struggling adolescents in low-performing schools need narratives that render them as competent learners with important work to do in the world, set in schools built to support their education, filled with characters who believe they will succeed (Perry, Steele, & Hilliard, 2003). The symbolic power of language is a potent tool for equity and excellence.

Creating Motivating Classrooms. Of course, talking the talk only gets us so far unless we also walk the walk. Schools organized for equity and excellence not only defuse stereotypes and counteract pervasive narratives of underachievement, they also create learning environments that reflect the possibilities embedded in these counternarratives. Creating motivating classrooms is critically important if we expect students to truly engage in deeper learning or rise to meet the greater demands of the Common Core State Standards. Teachers support students' motivation to learn by demonstrating care for their well-being and commitment to their learning. My 14 student participants were more inclined to engage in academic work when teachers encouraged them and provided feedback that drew attention to what they were doing well or conveyed confidence in their abilities to get it right the next time. Students applied themselves when teachers set clear expectations for assignments and helped equip students to proceed. Students were more motivated to work hard when they felt teachers were paying attention to whether they understood the material and provided support if they got stuck, without getting angry or frustrated. Finally, teachers supported students' motivation to learn when they made learning engaging, interactive, and relevant to their interests, with more emphasis on students' active participation and production and less time on teachers talking. The 14 students passed classes where teachers offered these supports. How might their overall trajectory in high school have been different if *all* their teachers had created such motivating classrooms?

Removing the Threat of Failure. Supporting students' motivation to learn could likely prevent a large number of course failures in urban high schools. But *preventing* course failures is not enough. Addressing the psychology of failure also means reframing failure altogether, encouraging risks, and normalizing small defeats, as students attempt to learn new things. As Dawson said about the biology teacher who gave him an F for a wrong hypothesis, "He could have gave me at least half credit for trying." When every piece of student work is graded and averaged into a final course grade, students have no space to take the risks inherent in learning; there is little incentive to try if you are pretty sure you won't get it right and know you will be penalized for getting it wrong.

College math professor Edward Burger requires his students to fail if they want an A in his class: 5% of students' final grade is based on their "quality of failure," meaning how well they analyze and learn from their wrong answers throughout the course. Since implementing this policy, Burger found that students "gleefully take more risks and energetically engage in discussions." He gave this example:

> After returning a graded assignment and reviewing the more challenging questions, I ask students to share their errors—and the class immediately comes to life: everyone wants to show off their mistakes as they now know they are offering valuable learning moments. What's more, in this receptive atmosphere, it's actually fun to reveal those promising gems of an idea that turned out to be counterfeit. (Burger, 2012, n.p.)

By removing the material costs of making errors—in Professor Burger's case, in fact, rewarding mistakes—teachers can create strongly motivating classrooms that unleash students' intellectual curiosity. Schools structured for equity and excellence intentionally create environments that encourage students to take intellectual risks and analyze what goes wrong if they fail. This is how people learn! The greater the academic demands, the more essential risk-taking and error analysis become. Highlighting mistakes helps students uncover misconceptions and ensures that their understanding is built on a solid foundation. But young people will only embrace their mistakes if we don't penalize students for making them.

Students also need opportunities for "safe" practice when learning new skills, without being evaluated before they have developed competence. Soccer coaches don't grade players for their performance on each drill in every practice session. Instead, good coaches run drills over and over, providing feedback, giving players the opportunity to make mistakes and make corrections, and then practice, practice, practice until doing it right becomes habitual. This prepares players to do their best in games where performance really counts. Our routine failure to create such environments in high school classrooms probably goes a long way toward explaining why so many students leave school without having developed real academic competence.

Designing schools for equity and excellence requires a deep understanding of human learning as situated in a stratified society. Racial stereotypes permeate life in the United States, and we seem unendingly focused on racial "achievement gaps." The lived experience of urban students is often, as Jonathan Kozol (2005) put it, one of "apartheid schooling," where kids in low-level classes and detention halls have darker skin than the kids in AP courses, and the National Merit Scholars pictured in the local newspaper are predominantly White or Asian. The Latino and Black kids are all in "failing" schools with one another, while the wealthier, Whiter kids in their city go to better schools with higher-performing peers. As such, urban educators cannot afford to be color blind. Regardless of race or ethnicity, all students need to belong to vibrant school and classroom communities focused on intellectual achievement. Black and Latino students need those communities to consciously support healthy identity development, where intellectual achievement becomes an integral part of what it means to be a young person of color.

Research provides clear direction about how to create classrooms that support effort and motivation, particularly for the youth most grossly underserved in today's public high schools. In the context of the Common Core, addressing the motivational dimension of academic achievement means helping students interpret small failures not as shameful indications of academic deficiency, but as "no cost" opportunities for useful feedback to improve performance. Lastly, addressing the motivational dimension of achievement means helping students build strong and healthy academic identities that embrace intellectual risk-taking and provide a compelling counternarrative to negative stereotypes that bind up students' academic potential.

Building Students' Capacity to Achieve

Schools designed for equity and excellence must also address the developmental dimensions of student achievement. If adolescents are to meet increasing academic demands in high school, they need to develop new habits, skills, and strategies. For my 14 failing students, a major obstacle to improving their performance was that they didn't actually know what to do differently. They realized that academic behaviors such as taking notes, organizing their work, studying for tests, and completing homework were important, but they didn't know how to *make themselves* do any of these things. The good news is that doing well in school may depend more on strategy than on sheer willpower. Building capacity means teaching students explicit strategies for learning and for engaging in good academic behaviors.

Developing a Repertoire of Strategies. Students need academic strategies to tackle assignments, manage their workload, monitor their learning, and transfer content to long-term memory. Students with a repertoire of content-specific strategies, self-regulation strategies, and metacognitive strategies are better equipped—and hence more motivated—to work hard and persevere in the face of difficulty. Their efficient investments in reading or studying yield tangible results. Having effective strategies gives students more control over their learning and reinforces the mindsets that ability grows with effort and success is possible. Building students' capacity to learn means teaching them *how to* develop positive academic habits and effective learning strategies.

For the most part, teachers can easily incorporate such strategies into their regular lesson plans. For example, when giving a homework assignment, teachers could not only ensure that every student writes it down in a planner, but could ask students to envision precisely *when and where* they intend to complete the assignment. To take it a step further, teachers could ask students to identify an obstacle likely to prevent them from finishing their homework, and to make a plan for how they could get it done even if this obstacle arises. The next day, in addition to sharing their homework results, students could also share their strategies for completing it. Researchers have found that asking people to create mental images of accomplishing tasks and plans for overcoming obstacles significantly increases the likelihood of successful task completion (Duckworth, Grant, Loew, Oettingen, & Gollwitzer, 2010). Teachers could teach this strategy to students to help them fulfill their own good intentions.

Freshman year is a critical time for teaching adolescents to become effective learners and self-managers. This is not to discount the critical importance of content knowledge, but rather to emphasize that students won't learn content unless teachers explicitly coach them in the *process* of learning. As experts in their content areas, teachers need to apprentice students into expert ways of thinking and doing. How do mathematicians think about problem solving? How do historians get to the "truth" amid conflicting perspectives? How do readers know when they are confused, and how do they respond to their confusion? How do adults manage their time so that critical things get done? These all involve strategies that should be made explicit to and repeatedly demonstrated for young learners.

To accomplish this, educators need to let go of some old notions. When students enter high school with poor academic behaviors, we have to interrupt the perception of these behaviors as evidence of student character defects or moral failings. Rather than getting indignant if 14-year-olds can't manage their time or complete assignments, teachers would be better served by recognizing the radical nature of the transition to high school and the radical developmental period that is adolescence. In Chicago, most 8th-graders attend K–8 schools where their every move is tightly regulated. Teachers walk 13-year-olds from one room to another in straight and silent lines. If students miss something in class, they can ask for help from 30 peers and one main teacher they know well.

Suddenly, in 9th grade, students have multiple teachers, each with different expectations. High school students can wander the halls or walk out the school doors altogether; nobody seems to pay attention. Their teachers don't know them, and most of their classmates are strangers. Ninth-graders are left to handle every aspect of being a high school student on their own. This coincides with a developmental period of emerging independence that manifests itself by testing limits. When kids mess up—as they inevitably do—teachers get exasperated and start handing out Fs and admonitions. It is often at these moments that racial/ethnic stereotypes and narratives of deficiency influence teachers' responses to children's behavior: To whom do we give the benefit of the doubt? Unfortunately, students don't learn to develop effective learning strategies and academic behaviors through punishment, shame, or failure, any more than they learn geometry by those means.

High school teachers working for equity and excellence *must* believe in the intellectual abilities of their students and *must* take on the mission of building students' capacity as independent learners; there is nobody else waiting in the wings for young people who need this most. Kids need explicit instruction about habits and strategies. And just as with the development of content knowledge or academic skills, they need repeated modeling of learning strategies in action; lots of opportunity for "safe" practice to develop their competence in using new strategies; and ongoing, constructive feedback from caring adults as they develop their capacity to learn.

Expanding Students' Competence

Teaching for equity and excellence also means expanding students' competence by aggressively building content knowledge and skills. Princeton University professor Angel Harris analyzed extensive evidence around the hypothesis that Black youth took an "oppositional" stance in school because they associated academic achievement with "acting White." In his book *Kids Don't Want to Fail,* Harris concluded that many Black students performed poorly in school not because they rejected school or devalued education, but because they lacked the skills to succeed.

As the National Task Force on Minority High Achievement noted, the frontier of civil rights in education is not about access, but about the "affirmative development of academic ability" through "early and continued exposure to pleasurable and progressively more rigorous learning experiences"; the acquisition of factual knowledge and development of cognitive maps for organizing such knowledge; instruction in the learner's zone of proximal development; socialization to the demands of academic work; and repeated exposure to models of exemplary work (Gordon & Bridglall, 2006, pp. 67–68). In short, addressing the academic dimension of student achievement means teaching students how to learn and creating opportunities to significantly expand their knowledge and skills.

Low skills do not indicate anything about students' intellectual capacity. If students come into high school without sufficient background knowledge and understanding, well, school is a good place for them to be. Teach them what they need to know. A common mistake, however, is to focus explicitly on discrete low-level skills, assuming students need to learn these basics *before* they can engage in deep thinking about rich content. Schools focused on equity and excellence instead engage students immediately in real and compelling problems that give students reason to want to develop the skills to dig deeper in the work. Complex and meaningful work with sufficient scaffolding is always better than dry, low-level work that reinforces the idea that kids don't have the capacity for harder stuff. Here again, the Common Core State Standards provide a good map for the content and skills students should develop through their high school coursework. Equity and excellence demand that teachers focus on learning how to support every student to engage in challenging intellectual work to meet these standards.

Structuring Opportunities for Student Success

Realizing a new vision for public high schools also requires taking on the structural dimension of student achievement. I am convinced that equity and excellence for *all* students in urban public schools cannot be achieved in the absence of a radical restructuring of secondary education. Preventing massive failure requires that we move away from high schools designed to stratify achievement, and build an entirely new architecture of opportunity.

Drawing from historical and present-day examples, as well as a long line of research and empirical observation, I see three essential features of such an architecture. The first would be a standards-based grading and credit system, similar to what was in place at Devon High School or what is being put in place in states like Connecticut. Next would be structured opportunities for remediation and extension built into the regular school day and school calendar, so students could revisit material or receive additional instruction as needed to improve their academic performance. The third would be a dynamic transcript that recorded students' best work overall.

Standards-Based Grading and Credit Systems. Traditional structures and policies at Maxwell and Alexander high schools seriously constrained the ability of students to remediate their learning. Students couldn't catch up and earn a passing grade once they started failing a class, either because they didn't have sufficient opportunity to learn past material or because their early bad grades overwhelmed their later, better grades. Largely, this boiled down to classroom policies that discounted the value of late work, entered zeros for missing assignments, and averaged all assignments across a term to obtain a final grade. Students could never outrun a stretch of poor performance and received no "grace period" for figuring things out.

Traditional structures and policies also interfered with students' ability to earn lost credit after failing a class. Credits were tied to time, and recovering credit required investing an additional term to retake each failed course. At some point, dropping out of school seemed rational within this system, as 17-year-olds realized they were still years away from earning enough credits to graduate.

Designing schools for equity and excellence requires decoupling time and credits. Instead of earning credit for a passing grade on a semester's work, students would earn credits by demonstrating competency in specific learning goals, for example by meeting Common Core State Standards for their grade level (or other applicable academic standards, as determined by their school), regardless of the time it took to do so. Schools could get creative about how they organized instructional units within a school calendar.

Rather than rigidly dividing students into grade levels and time into quarters or semesters, flexible groupings could allow students to move on to new material or loop back for more instruction, depending on their level of proficiency. Project-based units provide additional flexibility, giving students the opportunity to focus on the skills they most need to improve. Students could finish high school in anywhere from 3 to 5 years, depending on their needs and interests. But every graduate would have gotten there by demonstrating that he learned what he was supposed to learn, and nobody would waste time waiting to fail just to retake a course from the beginning.

Standards-based grading and credit systems (also called competency-based systems) would also rectify a longstanding irony. Though American schools have operated under standards-based accountability for almost 3 decades, high schools themselves have done little to become truly standards-based in their organization. For example, in most schools and classrooms there are no records of which students have met which state standards. Teachers plan and teach in terms of content, not standards. They assess students' performance through homework, quizzes, projects, papers, and the like for a content-based unit, and organize their grades accordingly. To encourage students to turn in assignments, teachers often give full credit for timely completion, regardless of quality or accuracy. They give "extra credit" points for any number of unrelated activities. As a result, students' course grades can be entirely disconnected from their mastery of standards.

This prevailing approach sends an unfortunate message about the purpose of school. Students come to believe grades are a function of the height of their stack of work rather than what that work reveals about their knowledge and skills or the quality of their thinking. Students' de facto goal becomes piling up assignments to earn passing grades and accumulate credits rather than broadening knowledge, sharpening skills, deepening understanding, or making substantive contributions. When piling up work or earning credits begins to look like a losing proposition, students see little point to being in school.

To ensure equity and excellence for all students, schools must restructure themselves around what is important. Standards-based grading and credit policies put student learning at the center of the system. Schools can then structure instructional opportunities to ensure that every student learns what is important to know. A standards-based high school could: (1) clearly articulate essential knowledge and skills as learning goals; (2) organize classrooms so students could practice those skills and develop that knowledge; (3) assess and record student performance relative to each learning goal; (4) target remediation efforts and enrichment opportunities so students got exactly the help they needed when they needed it to meet the goals; and (5) award credit—and ultimately grant diplomas—on the basis of demonstrated knowledge and skills. Adoption of the Common Core Standards presents an exceptional opportunity to create competency-based high schools organized to ensure student learning rather than to stratify student achievement.

Structured Opportunities to Learn Past Material. Equitable and excellent schools give students the necessary time and support to learn what they need to know and provide structured opportunities for students to revisit material they did not initially master. This is where the structural, academic, developmental, and motivational dimensions of student achievement come together. Unfortunately, in most high schools, attempts to remediate learning are unconvincing on all four fronts. Rather than demonstrating an institutional commitment to student success by structuring necessary supports as an integrated part of schooling, such support is often isolated, haphazard, optional, and half-hearted. Although many schools have tutoring programs, for example, these services are often provided by volunteer organizations or noninstructional staff with little or no direct link to students' classrooms. Teachers may volunteer to assist students before or after school, but often this goes above and beyond their contractual duties. Structured opportunities for student remediation may be in place, but they are tenuous.

Tutoring programs and other remedial services are generally voluntary on the part of the student, too. Unfortunately, in a context where having to put in extra effort is generally taken as a sign that one isn't "smart," few students volunteer to single themselves out as needing extra help. Students might also doubt that tutoring will be helpful—particularly if they've diagnosed their problem as "just needing to try harder" rather than not understanding the material. Unfortunately, school personnel don't always recognize all the reasons that students avoid tutoring. Instead, the "failure" of struggling students to seek out and use available supports is often taken as further evidence that kids don't care about school.

Devon High School structured a whole system of opportunities and supports for remediation and credit recovery, and it serves as a good exemplar here. For each class, students could get a list of their unmet learning outcomes—their own list of things to learn—available online, updated daily. Students attended daily advisory periods where a caring adult reviewed their *Not Yet* lists and monitored their progress on these learning outcomes. The school structured opportunities for students to meet with teachers 3 days each week outside of class (two academic workshops and Saturday school) and required teachers to attend at least one such weekly session as part of their regular duties. When students did additional work and could demonstrate the specified knowledge and skills, teachers overrode their previous grade, providing immediate reinforcement for students' efforts.

Moreover, because Devon kept a database of students' met and unmet learning outcomes, teachers always knew exactly who still needed to learn what. The biology teacher knew which of her current students were still struggling with cell structure and she could re-teach that as needed. The geometry teacher could print a list of all students in the school who had not yet mastered sine and cosine, and he could send targeted invitations for after-school sessions on that topic. Using data on unmet outcomes, summer school was similarly organized into specific weeks devoted to specified topics, and students only attended school for the weeks they needed.

The efficiency of this system allowed failing students at Devon High School to earn passing grades and recover credits much more quickly than their peers in Maxwell and Alexander, as it reinforced their motivation to keep working. Students graduated from Devon only after meeting a remarkably high standard: they had to demonstrate proficiency in 85% of what they were taught across all their high school classes. And even though the bar to graduate was substantially higher at Devon than in regular CPS schools, Devon had a graduation rate that was, on average, over 15% higher than the rest of the district. By structuring systems of opportunity around student learning goals, equitable and excellent schools make it possible for even struggling students to meet ambitious academic standards.

Dynamic Transcripts. Traditional academic transcripts seal the deal on the stratification function of high schools. Students with consistently high grades can cash in for better colleges, more scholarships, better jobs, even lower car insurance rates. No doubt the rationale for the traditional transcript is to provide an "objective" picture of a student's performance across 4 years of high school. As critiqued in Chapter 2, however, transcripts employ a peculiar kind of objectivity. They shine light on students' successes and failures as individual accomplishments but obscure the very real material conditions that gave rise to them and the motivational, academic, developmental, and structural dimensions of their varying schooling experiences.

Social psychologists have demonstrated that stereotype threat, for example, depresses the academic performance of African American students such that traditional cognitive assessments systematically underestimate their knowledge and skills. In brief interventions designed to counteract stereotype threat, the boost to students' grades was consistently about one-third of a grade point—the size of the difference between C-plus and B-minus. This suggests that Black students' grades may well be artificially lower than they should be, or than they would be if they possessed the exact same knowledge and skills, but were White or Asian. Rather than being reliable measures, grades recorded on a transcript may systematically mischaracterize student achievement.

In addition to the problem of systematic bias, transcripts also record systemic inequities. A student from a well-educated family entering 9th grade from a well-resourced elementary or middle school will bring knowledge and skills that give her advantages over a classmate who enters without that past background and experience. Even if the two students are equally smart and work equally hard, the student entering with advantages will be able to draw on her cumulative academic resources to earn a higher grade. This process would repeat every year, culminating in two very different high school GPAs. Once students have an academic advantage, that advantage is perpetuated and legitimated by static transcripts.

Schools would go a long way in eliminating this systematic bias by restructuring transcripts to become dynamic documents. Students with subpar performance would have the option of doing more work to improve their recorded grade. They may enter a school or classroom with disadvantages, but they would be able to set the record straight by demonstrating higher performance over time. Of course, this could only happen if students put in additional effort. And here's where this is a radical concept. Dynamic transcripts would provide incentive for students to work hard and learn more—the primary aim of schools structured for equity and excellence—rather than penalizing them for preexisting skill and knowledge deficits.

Some who cling to the notion of objectivity might think this is unfair, that to override a failing grade, for example, does not paint an accurate picture of a student's high school performance. I would argue that dynamic transcripts are quite accurate records. The only difference is that they reflect a student's cumulative accomplishments over 4 years rather than at fixed time points along the way. Dynamic transcripts make it theoretically possible for every high school student to graduate with a 4.0 GPA. Regardless of their initial grades, students could continue working until they mastered everything they were taught. If you are having a visceral reaction to that idea—*how could colleges or employers tell students apart if everybody had 4.0s?*—you might now pause and reflect on the degree to which the stratification and selection function of high schools has become so taken for granted. Imagine a school where everyone worked hard enough to learn everything they were taught. Not only would that be a phenomenal victory for public education, but it would serve us much better than a system that "accurately" differentiated between winners and losers. I would urge us to use this better vision to guide our work forward.

REDESIGNING URBAN HIGH SCHOOLS FOR THE 21ST CENTURY

The 19th-century American high school was designed to create winners and losers, and it has done that very, very well. But we now stand with both feet firmly in a very different century, and that design no longer serves us. As we face not only persistent but *rising* inequality and new environmental, social, and technological challenges, we need to ensure that our children receive the kind of education that will allow each of them to reach their utmost potential and contribute to the solving of 21st-century problems. This is particularly true for youth in communities most devastated by high rates of academic failure and dropout. We simply cannot afford to proceed with business as usual. Without some radical change in high schools, despite our best intentions and all our efforts to the contrary, our well-worn structures, policies, and practices will continue to function the way they always have: to sort, to cull, to winnow, to waste.

I have tried to show here that overcoming high school failure is not a simple matter of individual volition. It requires addressing a complex structural problem. This does not mean we are doomed to repeat the past. Learning failures need not signify the end of opportunity, and high schools need not be sites for reproducing social inequality. We can disconnect failure from the devastating chain of consequences we have constructed and create some real alternatives. But to do this, we must change the system that guarantees our current results.

By reflecting on the past history of secondary education, we can learn from our failure. By drawing on our collective knowledge, we can fashion new possibilities. We can design schools that support students' motivation, build their capacity, expand their competence, and structure opportunities for continued learning. By being bold and courageous, we can create truly equitable and excellent urban American high schools—schools that prepare children and youth to engage productively in the world, lead fulfilling lives, contribute to the greater good, and go forward confidently into their futures. We are in desperate need of their help as we face the challenges and embrace the opportunities ahead.

Notes

Chapter 1

1. Using the monolithic category of "Asian" misrepresents the experience of many Asian students within that category. Chinese, Korean, and Japanese Americans tend to have much higher achievement and better educational outcomes than more recent Southeast Asian immigrant groups (Cheng & Yang, 2000; Yang, 2004). Unfortunately, most national databases do not disaggregate the category of "Asian" and, as one group in aggregate, Asian students tend to post high academic achievement relative to both Whites and other minority groups. Because of the small percentage of Native American students in large urban school systems and the lack of disaggregated data for Asian students, I focus primarily on comparisons of African American, Latino, and White youth.

Chapter 2

1. Historical enrollment data cited by the U.S. Department of Health, Education, and Welfare, Office of Education, in 1960 showed a slightly higher graduation rate at the turn of the century. The *Biennial Survey of Education in the United States* reported that 6.7% of persons aged 14–17 were enrolled in high school in 1889–1890, and that 3.5% of persons 17 years of age had graduated from public and non-public high schools in that year. Statistics cited in Hahn & Bidna, 1965, pp. 84–85.

2. *Laggards* is a term used by Leonard Ayres (1909) in reference to the students who progressed more slowly through school than a grade per year. Ayres, however, did not share the view that schools were intended to winnow out such students. Instead, he drew attention to the large numbers of students over age for grade or eliminated entirely from the system with each passing year. He saw this as a sign of the mismatch between the structure of schools and the needs of many students.

3. A previous version of this review and the arguments contained within first appeared in Farrington & Small, 2008. Portions are reprinted here by permission of the authors.

4. British sociologist Michael Young invented the word *meritocracy* in a satirical book, *The Rise of the Meritocracy,* originally published in 1958. In a new introduction in 1994, he noted that very few people got the joke. He attempted to present arguments both for and against a meritocratic system. Clearly, meritocracy was a

better way to determine political power and social privilege than aristocracy or plutocracy or nepotism, but Young's book was also written as a cautionary tale: "If the rich and powerful were encouraged by the general culture to believe that they fully deserved all they had, how arrogant they could become, and, if they were convinced it was all for the common good, how ruthless in pursuing their own advantage" (p. xvi). Young's primary concern was that "ordinary people" who had been "rejected by the educational system," and thus "think themselves inferior" to those with power, would not have the "confidence to assert themselves against the mighty" (p. xvi).

5. Enrollment numbers cited came from publicly available data from the Chicago Public Schools website, FY12_Racial_Ethnic_Survey.xls. Available at http://www.cps.edu/SchoolData/Pages/SchoolData.aspx.

Chapter 3

1. Examples of intervention studies targeting academic mindsets include: (1) Wilson and Linville's (1982, 1985) study of college students who were exposed to short videos of upperclassmen describing their freshman-year experiences in college. A year after the intervention, students who saw videos normalizing the difficulty of freshman year (older students saying their grades started out low but got better over time) had earned higher college grades (0.27 grade points) and were significantly less likely to have dropped out of school compared with a control group who saw a different video; (2) Blackwell, Trzesniewski, and Dweck's (2007) study of African American and Latino 7th-graders who participated in an 8-week after-school session that taught them that the brain was like a muscle and got stronger with use. At the end of the school year, participants had higher math grades (0.30 grade points) than the control group who received math tutoring during the same time period; and (3) Walton & Cohen's (2007, 2011) study of Black and White college students who read a survey showing that it was normal for students to feel like they did not belong when they first went to college. Students then wrote a speech explaining the survey results to others. Black students who received the intervention earned higher GPAs (0.24 grade points) from sophomore through senior years and were more likely to be in the top of their class than Black students in the control group. See Yeager & Walton (2011) for a full review of this research.

2. I want to distinguish here between the concept of academic achievement being congruent with one's social identities, as described in this chapter, and the concept of categorizing academic achievement as "acting White." There is little evidence that African American teenagers value educational achievement any less than any other group of teenagers (Toldson & Owens, 2010) or that they equate academic success with Whiteness. To say that minority students may experience their racial/ethnic identity as being inconsistent with academic achievement is not to imply that minority youth do not *value* education or *aspire* to be academic achievers, but rather that they are bombarded by implicit and explicit social messages about their cultural

group's *lack* of academic achievement. African American, Latino, and Native American youth growing up in the early 21st century are likely to attend schools preoccupied with "achievement gaps" and the relative performance of various racial/ethnic subgroups on standardized tests. They grow up believing that no one *expects them* to do well in school, regardless of their own values and aspirations.

Chapter 4

1. Devon High is a school I knew very well prior to this study. I was directly involved in the development of Devon's alternative student evaluation system and knew that Devon had worked very purposefully to create policies and practices that would respond differently to student failure. At the time of the pilot study, I had no formal ties to Devon High School. Although I knew the administrators and some of the teachers, I did not know any of the students I interviewed, and they did not know that I had any previous relationship with the school or had any knowledge of how its alternative grading system worked. Though I would not claim "objectivity," I did enter this research with an open stance toward understanding how students experienced this alternative system. I intentionally asked questions in all of my interviews that challenged both my assumptions and my previous experience with Devon's grading system.

2. I recruited and received consent for five Alexander students initially—which were all the freshmen from the entering cohort of fall 2005 who met the inclusion criteria. Before I began interviews, one student notified me (and the school) that she was pregnant and subsequently transferred to a Chicago high school for pregnant teens. Another student stopped attending school altogether before I collected any data, bringing my number of consented participants down to three.

3. I also had prior knowledge of Alexander High School. I had served the school on a consultancy basis in its early years. In this capacity I had free rein to observe classes, talk with students and teachers, analyze student work, and review policy documents. I also had an ongoing professional relationship with the principal through various local educational associations. This gave me a baseline of knowledge about and degree of access to Alexander that I would not have otherwise had. My impressions going into Alexander were of a young school with a committed staff dedicated to "getting it right," yet struggling against the odds created by racial oppression and economic injustice that were part and parcel of working in urban education.

Chapter 5

1. The graph appears in Allensworth and Easton's (2007) CCSR report, *What Matters for Staying On-Track and Graduating in Chicago Public High Schools*. Figure 5 on page 7 of that report shows the relationship between 4-year high school

graduation rates and freshman absence rates. For example, 87% of freshmen with 0–4 days absent per semester ended up graduating from high school in 4 years. When freshman absences increased to 5–9 days per semester, the percentage of graduates dropped to 63%. Students with 10–14 days absent graduated at a rate of 41%. After 14 days, the graduation rate dropped by half for every additional 4 days of absence.

References

Ahmed-Ullah, N. S. (2012, March 3). A really brutal admissions year. *Chicago Tribune*. Available at http://articles.chicagotribune.com/2012-03-03/news/ct-met-cps-selective-20120302_1_seventh-grade-academic-scores-socioeconomic-tiers-selective-enrollment.

Aikin, W. M. (1942). *The story of the eight-year study*. Adventures in American Education, Vol. 1. New York, NY: Harper & Brothers.

Allensworth, E. M., & Easton, J. Q. (2007). *What matters for staying on-track and graduating in Chicago public high schools: A close look at course grades, failures, and attendance in the freshman year*. Chicago, IL: University of Chicago, Consortium on Chicago School Research.

Alliance for Excellent Education. (2011, May). *A time for deeper learning: Preparing students for a changing world*. Policy Brief. Washington, DC: Author.

Another suicide by carbolic acid. (1895, June 30). *Chicago Daily Tribune*, p. 2.

Aronson, J., Cohen, G., & McColskey, W. (2009). *Reducing stereotype threat in classrooms: A review of social-psychological intervention studies on improving the achievement of Black students* (Regional Education Laboratory, REL 2009-086). Washington, DC: U.S. Department of Education, Institute for Education Science, National Center for Education Evaluation and Regional Assistance.

Assessment Reform Group. (2002). *Testing, motivation and learning*. Cambridge, UK: University of Cambridge Faculty of Education.

Atkinson, J. W. (1957). Motivational determinants of risk-taking behavior. *Psychological Review, 64*, 359–372.

Ayres, L. P. (1909). *Laggards in our schools: A study of retardation and elimination in city school systems*. Philadelphia, PA: Russell Sage Foundation.

Bandura, A. (1986). *Social foundations of thought and action: A social cognitive theory*. Englewood Cliffs, NJ: Prentice Hall.

Bandura, A., & Schunk, D. H. (1981). Cultivating competence, self-efficacy, and intrinsic interest through proximal self-motivation. *Journal of Personality and Social Psychology, 41*, 586–598.

Barker, A. C. (1903/1965). Extent and causes of pupils dropping out of the high school. *High School Association*, December 13, 1903, pp. 17–21. Reprinted in R. O. Hahn & D. B. Bidna (Eds.), (1965), *Secondary education: Origins and directions* (pp. 79–81). New York, NY: Macmillan.

Battistich, V., Solomon, D., Kim, D., Watson, M., & Schaps, E. (1995). Schools as communities, poverty levels of student populations, and students' attitudes, motives, and performance: A multilevel analysis. *American Educational Research Journal, 32*(3), 627–658.

Berger, P. L., & Luckmann, T. (1966). *The social construction of reality: A treatise in the sociology of knowledge.* New York, NY: Anchor.

Berkeley teachers to whip unruly pupils. (1907, July 11). *The San Francisco Call, 102*(41), 7.

Berliner, D. C. (2006). Our impoverished view of educational reform. *Teachers College Record, 108*(6), 949–995.

Berliner, D. C. (2009, March). *Poverty and potential: Out-of-school factors and school success.* Boulder, CO and Tempe, AZ: Education and the Public Interest Center & Education Policy Research Unit. Available at http://epicpolicy.org/publication/poverty-and-potential

Black, P., & Wiliam, D. (2004). The formative purpose: Assessment must first promote learning. In M. Wilson (Ed.), *Toward coherence between classroom assessment and accountability. 103rd Yearbook of the National Society for the Study of Education* (pp. 20–50). Chicago, IL: University of Chicago Press.

Blackwell, L. S., Trzesniewski, K. H., & Dweck, C. S. (2007). Implicit theories of intelligence predict achievement across an adolescent transition: A longitudinal study and an intervention. *Child Development, 78*(1), 246–263.

Blascovich, J., Spencer, S. J., Quinn, D. M., & Steele, C. M. (2001). African Americans and high blood pressure: The role of stereotype threat. *Psychological Science, 13*(3), 225–229.

Bloom, B. S. (1968). Learning for mastery. *Evaluation Comment, 1,* 1–5.

Bouffard-Bouchard, T. (1990). Influence of self-efficacy on performance in a cognitive task. *Journal of Social Psychology, 130,* 353–363.

Bowen, W. G., Chingos, M. M., & McPherson, M. S. (2009). *Crossing the finish line: Completing college at America's public universities.* Princeton, NJ: Princeton University Press.

Bowles, S., & Gintis, H. (1976). *Schooling in capitalist America: Educational reform and the contradictions of economic life.* New York, NY: Basic Books.

Brookhard, S. M. (2004). *Grading.* Upper Saddle River, NJ: Pearson Education, Inc.

Bruner, J. S. (1960). *The process of education.* Cambridge, MA: Harvard University Press.

Burger, E. (2012). Essay on the importance of teaching failure. *Inside Higher Ed.* Available at http://www.insidehighered.com/views/2012/08/21/essay-importance-teaching-failure

Carroll, J. (1963, May). A model of school learning. *Teachers College Record, 64,* 723–733.

Cheng, L., & Yang, P. Q. (2000). The "model minority" deconstructed. In M. Zhou & J. V. Gatewood (Eds.), *Contemporary Asian America: A multidisciplinary reader* (pp. 459–482). New York, NY: New York University Press.

Cohen, G. L., & Garcia, J. (2008). Identity, belonging, and achievement: A model, interventions, implications. *Current Directions in Psychological Science, 17*(6), 365–369.

Collins, A., & Smith, E. E. (1982). Teaching the process of reading comprehension. In D.K. Detterman & R.J. Sternberg (Eds.), *How much and how can intelligence be increased?* (pp. 173–185). Norwood, NJ: Ablex.

Connecticut Association of Public School Superintendents. (2012). *NextEd: Transforming Connecticut's education system.* West Hartford, CT: Author.

Covington, M. V., & Müeller, K. J. (2001). Intrinsic versus extrinsic motivation: An approach/avoidance reformulation. *Educational Psychology Review, 13,* 157–176.

Covington, M. V., & Teel, K. M. (1996). *Overcoming student failure: Changing motives and incentives for learning.* Washington, DC: American Psychological Association.

Croizet, J. C., & Dutrévis, M. (2004). Socioeconomic status and intelligence: Why test scores do not equal merit. *Journal of Poverty, 8*(3), 91–107.

Crooks, T. J. (1988). The impact of classroom evaluation practices on students. *Review of Educational Research, 58,* 438–481.

Cuban, L., & Shipps, D. (Eds.). (2000). *Reconstructing the common good in education: Coping with intractable American dilemmas.* New York, NY: Cambridge University Press.

Cubberley, E. P. (1919). *Public education in the United States.* Cambridge, MA: Riverside Press.

Cury, F., Elliott, A. J., Da Fonseca, D., & Moller, A. C. (2006). The social-cognitive model of achievement motivation and the 2 x 2 achievement goal framework. *Journal of Personality and Social Psychology, 90,* 666–679.

Csikszentmihalyi, M. (1990). *Flow: The psychology of optimal experience.* New York, NY: Harper & Row.

Damon, W. (2008). *The path to purpose: Helping our children find their calling in life.* New York, NY: The Free Press.

Department of the Interior. (1918). Bureau of Education, Bulletin No. 35. *Cardinal principles of secondary education.* A report of the Commission on the Reorganization of Secondary Education, appointed by the National Education Association. Washington, DC: United States Government Printing Office.

Deschenes, S., Tyack, D., & Cuban, L. (2001). Mismatch: Historical perspectives on schools and students who don't fit them. *Teachers College Record, 103,* 525–547.

Duckworth, A. L., Grant, H., Loew, B., Oettingen, G., & Gollwitzer, P. M. (2010). Self-regulation strategies improve self-discipline in adolescents: Benefits of mental contrasting and implementation intentions. *Educational Psychology, 31*(1), 17–26.

Dweck, C. S. (2006). *Mindset: The new psychology of success.* New York, NY: Ballantine Books.

Dweck, C. S., & Leggett, E. L. (1988). A social cognitive approach to motivation and personality. *Psychological Review, 95,* 256–273.

Ebel, R. L. (1980). The failure of schools without failure. *Phi Delta Kappan, 61,* 386–388.

Eccles, J. S., Adler, T. F., Futterman, R., Goff, S. B., Kaczala, C. M., Meece, J. L., & Midgley, C. (1983). Expectancies, values, and academic behaviors. In J. T. Spence (Ed.), *Achievement and achievement motivation* (pp. 75–146). San Francisco, CA: W. H. Freeman.

Eliot, C. W. (1909, April). Educational reform and the social order. *School Review, 17,* 217–222.

Espinoza-Herold, M. (2003). *Issues in Latino education: Race, school culture, and the politics of academic success.* Boston, MA: Pearson Education Group.

Farkas, G. (2003). Cognitive skills and noncognitive traits and behaviors in stratification processes. *Annual Review of Sociology, 29,* 541–562.

Farrell, E. (1990). *Hanging in and dropping out: Voices of at-risk high school students.* New York, NY: Teachers College Press.

Farrington, C. A., Roderick, M., Allensworth, E., Nagaoka, J., Keyes, T. S., Johnson, D. W., & Beechum, N. O. (2012). *Teaching adolescents to become learners: The role of noncognitive factors in shaping school performance: A critical literature review.* Chicago, IL: University of Chicago Consortium on Chicago School Research.

Farrington, C. A., & Small, M. H. (2008). *A new model of student assessment for the 21st century.* Washington, DC: American Youth Policy Forum.

Feather, N. T. (1999). *Values, achievement, and justice: Studies in the psychology of deservingness.* New York, NY: Kluwer Academic/Plenum.

Fenske, N. R. (1997). *A history of American public high schools 1890–1900: Through the eyes of principals.* Lewiston, NY: Edwin Mellen Press.

Fine, M. (1991). *Framing dropouts: Notes on the politics of an urban public high school.* Albany, NY: State University of New York Press.

Furrer, C., & Skinner, E. (2003). Sense of relatedness as a factor in children's academic engagement and performance. *Journal of Educational Psychology, 95,* 148–162.

Garner, R., & Alexander, P. (1989). Metacognition: Answered and unanswered questions. *Educational Psychologist, 24,* 143–158.

Geiser, S., & Santelices, M. V. (2007). *Validity of high-school grades in predicting student success beyond the freshman year: High-school record vs. standardized tests as indicators or four-year college outcomes.* Research & Occasional Paper Series: CSHE.6.07. Berkeley, CA: Center for Studies in Higher Education.

Goldin, C., & Katz, L. F. (2008). *The race between education and technology.* Cambridge, MA: Belknap Press.

Goldin, C., & Katz, L. F. (2009). The future of inequality: The other reason education matters so much. *Milken Institute Review,* 26–33.

Good, C., Aronson, J., & Inzlicht, M. (2003). Improving adolescents' standardized test performance: An intervention to reduce the effects of stereotype threat. *Journal of Applied Developmental Psychology, 24,* 645–662.

Goodenow, C., & Grady, K. E. (1993). The relationship of school belonging and friends' values to academic motivation among urban adolescent students. *Journal of Experimental Education, 2*(1), 60–71.

Gordon, E. W., & Bridglall, B. L. (2006). The affirmative development of academic ability: In pursuit of social justice. In A. F. Ball (Ed.), *With more deliberate speed: Achieving equity and excellence in education—Realizing the full potential of Brown v. Board of Education.* 105th Yearbook of the National Society for the Study of Education, Part 2 (pp. 58–68). Malden, MA: Blackwell Publishing.

Greene, J. (2001, November/rev. 2002, April). *Public school graduation rates in the United States* (Civic Rep. No. 31). New York, NY: Manhattan Institute for Policy Research.

Hahn, R. O., & Bidna, D. B. (Eds.). (1965). *Secondary education: Origins and directions.* New York, NY: Macmillan.

Haney, W. (2000, August 19). The myth of the Texas miracle in education. *Education Policy Analysis Archives, 8.* Available at http://epaa. asu.edu/epaa/ v8n41/

Harris, A. L. (2011). *Kids don't want to fail: Oppositional culture and the Black-White achievement gap.* Cambridge, MA: Harvard University Press.

Harvey, O. J., & Schroder, H. M. (1963). Cognitive aspects of self and motivation. In O. J. Harvey (Ed.), *Motivation and social interaction: Cognitive determinants* (pp. 95–133). New York, NY: The Ronald Press Co.

Hot day for educators: Lively row at the National Council at Milwaukee. (1897, July 6). *Chicago Daily Tribune,* p. 4.

Jayakody, R., Danziger, S. H., & Pollack, H. A. (2000). Mental health problems, substance abuse and welfare reform. *Journal of Health Politics, Policy and Law, 25,* 623–651.

Judd, C. S. (1914, December). Formalism in defining high-school units. *The School Review 22*(10), 649–665.

Junn, J. (2005, October). The political costs of unequal education. Paper prepared for the symposium on the Social Costs of Inadequate Education, Teachers College, Columbia University, New York, NY. Available at http://devweb.tc.columbia. edu/manager/symposium/Files/73_junn_paper.ed.pdf

Kaestle, C. F. (1983). *Pillars of the republic: Common schools and American society, 1780–1860.* New York, NY: Hill and Wang.

Kaplan, D. S., Peck, B. M., & Kaplan, H. B. (1997). Decomposing the academic failure-dropout relationship: A longitudinal analysis. *Journal of Educational Research, 90,* 331–343.

Kaplan, S., & Kaplan, R. (1982). *Cognition and environment: Functioning in an uncertain world.* New York, NY: Praeger.

Kelley, H. H. (1973). The process of causal attribution. *American Psychologist, 28,* 107–128.

King, A. J. C., Warren, W. K., Michalski, C., & Pearlt, M. J. (1988). *Improving student retention in Ontario secondary schools.* Toronto, Canada: Ministry of Education.

Koos, L. V. (1933, September). Trends in secondary-school programs of study. *The School Review, 41,* 507.

Kozol, J. (2005). *The shame of the nation: The restoration of apartheid schooling in America.* New York, NY: Crown.

Krendl, A. C., Richeson, J. A., Kelley, W. M., & Heatherton, T. F. (2008). The negative consequences of threat: A functional magnetic resonance imaging investigation of the neural mechanisms underlying women's underperformance in math. *Psychological Science, 19*(2), 168–175.

Labaree, D. F. (1988). *The making of an American high school: The credentials market and the Central High School of Philadelphia, 1838–1939.* New Haven, CT: Yale University Press.

Labaree, D. F. (1997). Public goods, private goods: The American struggle over educational goals. *American Educational Research Journal (34)* 1, 39–81.

Labov, W. (1982). Competing value systems in the inner city schools. In P. Gilmore & A. Glathorn (Eds.), *Children in and out of school: Ethnography and education* (pp. 148–171). Washington, DC: Center for Applied Linguistics.

Ladson-Billings, G. (1994). *The dreamkeepers: Successful teachers of African American children.* San Francisco, CA: Jossey-Bass.

Lawrence, B. (1965, May). *The Carnegie unit: An evaluation of its utility for secondary education achievement evaluation.* Special Bulletin. Eugene, OR: Oregon School Study Council.

Ledgerwood, A., Mandisodza, A. N., Jost, J. T., & Pohl, M. J. (2011). Working for the system: Motivated defense of meritocratic beliefs. *Social Cognition, 29*(2), 322–340.

Lee, V. E., & Burkam, D. T. (2002). *Inequality at the starting gate: Social background differences in achievement as children begin school.* Washington, DC: Economic Policy Institute.

Legters, N., Balfanz, R., Jordan, W., & McPartland, J. (2002). *Comprehensive reform for urban high schools: A Talent Development approach.* New York, NY: Teachers College Press.

Lent, R. W., Brown, S. D., & Larkin, K. C. (1984). Relation of self-efficacy expectations to academic achievement and persistence. *Journal of Counseling Psychology, 31,* 356–362.

Lester, F. K. Jr., Masingila, J. O., Mau, S. T., Lambdin, D. V., dos Santon, V. W., & Raymond, A. M. (1994). Learning how to teach via problem solving. In D. Aichele & A. Coxford (Eds.), *Professional development for teachers of mathematics* (pp. 152–166). Reston, VA: National Council of Teachers of Mathematics.

Lewontin, R. C. (1992). *Biology as ideology: The doctrine of DNA*. New York, NY: Harper Perennial.

Lister, R. (2006). Ladder of opportunity or engine of inequality? In G. Dench (Ed.), *The rise and rise of meritocracy* (pp. 232–236). Malden, MA: Blackwell and *Political Quarterly.*

Long, F. E. (1934, May). The high school in competition. *Journal of Educational Sociology, 7*(9), pp. 579–580.

Marks, H. M. (2000). Student engagement in instructional activity: Patterns in the elementary, middle, and high school years. *American Educational Research Journal, 37,* 153–184.

Markus, H., & Kunda, Z. (1986). Stability and malleability of the self-concept. *Journal of Personality and Social Psychology, 51,* 858–866.

Marshall, R. L. (2003). *The pivotal year: How freshman can become sophomores*. Lanham, MD: Scarecrow Press.

McClusky, F. D. (1920, Sept.). Introduction of grading into public school of New England, Part I. *The Elementary School Journal, 21,* 34–46.

McCombs, B. L. (1991). Motivation and lifelong learning. *Educational Psychologist, 26,* 117–127.

McCombs, B. L. (1993). Learner-centered psychological principles for enhancing education: Applications in school settings. In L. A. Penner, G. M. Batsche, H. M. Knoff, & D. L. Nelson (Eds.), *The challenges in mathematics and science education: Psychology's response* (pp. 287–313). Washington, DC: American Psychological Association.

McCombs, B. L. (1994). Strategies for assessing and enhancing motivation: Keys to promoting self-regulated learning and performance. In H. F. O'Neil, Jr., & M. Drillings (Eds.), *Motivation: Theory and research* (pp. 46–69). Hillsdale, NJ: Erlbaum.

McKnight, P. E., & Kashdan, T. B. (2009). Purpose in life as a system that creates and sustains health and well-being: An integrative, testable theory. *Review of General Psychology, 13,* 242–251.

McMillan, D. W., & Chavis, D. M. (1986). Sense of community: A definition and theory. *Journal of Community Psychology, 14*(January), 6–23.

MDRC. (2002). Fast fact archive. Available at http://www.mdrc.org/area_fact_9.html

Meyer, J. W., & Rowan, B. (1983). The structure of educational organizations. In J. W. Meyer & W. R. Scott (Eds.), *Organizational environments: Ritual and rationality* (pp. 71–97). Beverly Hills, CA: Sage.

Meyer, J. W., Scott, W. R., & Deal, T. E. (1983). Institutional and technical sources of organizational structure: Explaining the structure of educational organizations. In J. W. Meyer & W. R. Scott (Eds.), *Organizational environments: Ritual and rationality* (pp. 45–67). Beverly Hills, CA: Sage.

Meyer, M. (1908). The grading of students. *Science, 28*(712), 243–250.

Miller, S. R., Allensworth, E. M., & Kochanek, J. R. (2002, May). *Student performance: Course taking, test scores and outcomes: The state of Chicago public high school 1993 to 2000.* Chicago, IL: University of Chicago, Consortium on Chicago School Research. Available at http://www.consortium-chicago.org/publications/pdfs/p52.pdf

Moll, L. C., Amanti, C., Neff, D., & Gonzalez, N. (1992). Funds of knowledge for teaching: Using a qualitative approach to connect homes and classrooms. *Theory Into Practice, 31*(2), 132–141.

Muennig, P. (2005, October). The economic value of health gains associated with education interventions. Paper prepared for the symposium on the Social Costs of Inadequate Education, Teachers College, Columbia University, New York, NY. Available at http://devweb.tc.columbia.edu/manager/symposium/Files/75_Muennig_Executive%20Summary.pdf

National Research Council. (2002). *Learning and understanding: Improving advanced study of mathematics and science in U.S. high schools.* Committee on Programs for Advanced Study of Mathematics and Science in American High Schools. J. P. Gollub, M. W. Bertenthal, J. B. Labov, and P. C. Curtis, Editors. Center for Education, Division of Behavioral and Social Sciences and Education. Washington, DC: National Academy Press.

National Research Council. (2012). *Education for life and work: Developing transferable knowledge and skills in the 21st century.* Committee on Defining Deeper Learning and 21st Century Skills, J. W. Pellegrino and M. L. Hilton, Editors. Board on Testing and Assessment and Board on Science Education, Division of Behavioral and Social Sciences and Education. Washington, DC: The National Academies Press.

National Research Council and the Institute of Medicine. (2004). *Engaging schools: Fostering high school students' motivation to learn.* Washington, DC: National Academies Press.

Neild, R. C., & Weiss, C. C. (1999). *The Philadelphia Education Longitudinal Study (PELS): Report on the transition to high school in the school district of Philadelphia.* Philadelphia, PA: Philadelphia Education Fund.

No drones among them. (1896, March 13). *Chicago Daily Tribune,* p. 12.

Oakes, J., Wells, A. S., Jones, M., & Datnow, A. (1977). Detracking: The social construction of ability, cultural politics, and resistance to reform. *Teachers College Record, 98,* 482–510.

Oregon State Department of Education. (2000, April). *Dropout rates in Oregon high schools: 1998–99, State summary report.* Salem, OR: Author. Available at www.ode.state.or.us/stats

Osterman, K. F. (2000). Students' need for belonging in the school community. *Review of Educational Research, 70*(3), 323–367.

Oyserman, D. (2001). Self-concept and identity. In A. Tesser & N. Schwarz (Eds.), *The Blackwell handbook of social psychology* (pp. 499–517). Malden, MA: Blackwell.

Oyserman, D. (2008). Possible selves: Identity-based motivation and school success. In H. Marsh, R. G. Craven, & D. M. McInerney (Eds.), *Self-processes, learning, and enabling human potential* (pp. 269–288). Charlotte, NC: Information Age Publishing.

Oyserman, D., & Fryberg, S. (2006). The possible selves of diverse adolescents: Content and function across gender, race and national origin. In C. Dunkel & J. Kerpelman (Eds.), *Possible selves: Theory, research, and applications* (pp. 17–39). Hauppauge, NY: Nova Science Publishers.

Oyserman, D., & James, L. (2009). Possible selves: From content to process. In K. Markman, W. Klein, & J. A. Suhr (Eds.), *The handbook of imagination and mental stimulation* (pp. 373–394). New York, NY: Psychology Press.

Oyserman, D., & Markus, H. (1990). Possible selves in balance: Implications for delinquency. *Journal of Social Issues, 46,* 141–157.

Oyserman, D., & Markus, H. (1998). Self as social representation. In U. Flick (Ed.), *The psychology of the social* (pp. 107–125). New York, NY: Cambridge University Press.

Oyserman, D., Terry, K., & Bybee, D. (2002). A possible selves intervention to enhance school involvement. *Journal of Adolescence, 25,* 313–326.

Pajares, F. (1996). Self-efficacy beliefs in academic settings. *Review of Educational Research, 66,* 543–578.

Parker, F. W. (1902, June). An account of the work of the Cook County and Chicago Normal School from 1883 to 1899. *The Elementary School Teacher and Course of Study 2*(10).

Perry, T. (2003). Tackling the myth of Black students' intellectual inferiority. *Chronicle of Higher Education 49*(18), B10.

Perry, T., Steele, C., & Hilliard, III, A. (2003). *Young, gifted, and Black: Promoting high achievement among African American students.* Boston, MA: Beacon Press.

Pettit, B., & Western, B. (2001). Inequality in lifetime risks of incarceration. Paper presented at the meeting of the Population Association of America, Washington, DC.

Raphael, S. (2004). *The socioeconomic status of black males: The increasing importance of incarceration.* Berkeley, CA: Goldman School of Public Policy, University of California, Berkeley.

Reese, W. J. (1995). *The origins of the American high school.* New Haven, CT: Yale University Press.

Reese, W. J. (2005). *America's public schools: From the Common School to "No Child Left Behind."* Baltimore, MD: The Johns Hopkins University Press.

Resnick, L. B. (1995). From aptitude to effort: A new foundation for our schools. *Daedalus, 124*(3), 55–62.

Roderick, M., & Camburn, E. (1999). Risk and recovery from course failure in the early years of high school. *American Educational Research Journal, 36*(2), 303–343.

Roderick, M., Coca, V., Moeller, E., & Kelley-Kemple, T. (2013). *From high school to the future: The challenge of senior year in Chicago Public Schools.* Chicago, IL: University of Chicago Consortium on Chicago School Research.

Roderick, M., Kelley-Kemple, T., Johnson, D. W., & Beechum, N. O. (In press). *Raising graduation rates: Evaluating the impact of increasing 9th grade on-track rates in Chicago public schools.* Chicago, IL: University of Chicago, Consortium on Chicago School Research.

Roderick M., Nagaoka, J., & Allensworth E. (2006). *From high school to the future: A first look at Chicago public school graduates' college enrollment, college preparation, and graduation from four-year colleges.* Chicago, IL: University of Chicago, Consortium on Chicago School Research.

Rounds, C. R., & Kingsbury, H. B. (1913, November). Do too many students fail? *The School Review, 21*(9), 585–597.

Rouse, C. E. (2005, October). Labor market consequences of an inadequate education. Paper presented at the symposium on the Social Costs of Inadequate Education, Teachers College, Columbia University, New York, NY. Available at http://devweb.tc.columbia.edu/manager/symposium/Files/77_Rouse_paper.pdf

Schmader, T., & Johns, M. (2003). Convergent evidence that stereotype threat reduces working memory capacity. *Journal of Personality and Social Psychology, 85,* 440–452.

Schoenfeld, A. H. (1983). Problem solving in the mathematics curriculum: A report, recommendation and annotated bibliography. *Mathematical Association of America Notes,* (1).

Schoenfeld, A. H. (1985). *Mathematical problem solving.* Orlando, FL: Academic Press.

Schoenfeld, A. H. (1987). What's all the fuss about metacognition? In A. H. Schoenfeld (Ed.), *Cognitive science and mathematics education* (pp. 189–216). Hillside, NJ: Erlbaum.

Schunk, D. H., & Hanson, A. R. (1985). Peer models: Influence on children's self-efficacy and achievement. *Journal of Educational Psychology, 77,* 313–322.

Smyth, J., & Hattam, R. (2001). "Voiced" research as a sociology for understanding "dropping out" of school. *British Journal of Sociology of Education, 22,* 401–415.

Solomon, D., Watson, M., Battistich, V., Schaps, E., & Delucchi, K. (1996). Creating classrooms that students experience as communities. *American Journal of Community Psychology, 24*(6), 719–748.

Spady, W. (1992). On grades, grading and school reform. In J. A. Laska & T. Juarez (Eds.), *Grading and marking in American schools: Two centuries of debate* (pp. 67–76). Springfield, IL: Charles C Thomas Publisher.

Steele, C. M. (1997). A threat in the air: How stereotypes shape intellectual identity and performance. *American Psychologist, 52*, 613–629.

Steele, C. M. (2010). *Whistling Vivaldi: How stereotypes affect us and what we can do.* New York, NY: W. W. Norton & Co.

Steele, C. M., & Aronson, J. (1995). Stereotype threat and the intellectual test performance of African Americans. *Journal of Personality and Social Psychology, 69*(5), 797–811.

Strayer, G. D., & Engelhardt, N. L. (1920). *The classroom teacher at work in American schools.* New York, NY: American Book Company.

Swann, W. (1997). The trouble with change: Self-verification and allegiance to the self. *Psychological Science, 8*, 177–180.

Swanson, C. B. (2010, June 10). U.S. graduation rate continues decline. *Education Week, 29*(34), 22.

Toldson, I. A., & Owens, D. (2010). Editor's comment: "Acting Black": What Black kids think about being smart and other school-related experiences. *The Journal of Negro Education, 79*(2), 91–96.

Tompkins, E., & Gaumnitz, W. H. (1954). *The Carnegie Unit: Its origin, status, and trends.* U.S. Department of Health, Education, and Welfare, Office of Education, Bulletin No. 7. Washington, DC: U.S. Government Printing Office.

Too many poor pupils: High schools have children not fit to be there. (1896, March 19). *Chicago Daily Tribune*, p. 12.

Tough, P. (2012). *How children succeed: Grit, curiosity, and the hidden power of character.* New York, NY: Houghton Mifflin Harcourt.

Tyack, D. B. (1974). *The one best system: A history of American urban education.* Cambridge, MA: Harvard University Press.

U.S. Department of Education, National Center for Education Statistics. (2004). *The condition of education 2004.* Washington, DC: U.S. Government Printing Office, Indicator 16, p. 61.

Vispoel, W. P., & Austin, J. R. (1995). Success and failure in junior high school: A critical incident approach to understanding students' attributional beliefs. *American Educational Research Journal, 32*, 377–412.

Waldfogel, J., Garfinkel, I., & Kelly, B. (2005, October). Public assistance programs: How much could be saved with improved education? Paper presented at the symposium on The Social Costs of Inadequate Education, Teachers College, Columbia University, New York, NY. Available at http://devweb.tc.columbia.edu/manager/symposium/Files/79waldfogel _paper.ed.pdf

Walton, G. M., & Cohen, G. L. (2007). A question of belonging: Race, social fit, and achievement. *Journal of Personality and Social Psychology, 92*, 82–96.

Walton, G. M., & Cohen, G. L. (2011). A brief social-belonging intervention improves academic and health outcomes among minority students. *Science, 331,* 1447–1451.

Walton, G. M., & Spencer, S. J. (2009). Latent ability: Grades and test scores systematically underestimate the intellectual ability of negatively stereotyped students. *Psychological Science, 20*(9), 1132–1139.

Weiner, B. (1979). A theory of motivation for some classroom experiences. *Journal of Educational Psychology, 71,* 3–25.

Weiner, B. (1986). *An attributional theory of emotion and motivation.* New York, NY: Springer-Verlag.

Wentzel, K. R., & Caldwell, K. (1997). Friendships, peer acceptance, and group membership: Relations to academic achievement in middle school. *Child Development, 68*(6), 1198–1209.

West, T. C. (2009). *Still a freshman: Examining the prevalence and characteristics of ninth-grade retention across six states.* Baltimore, MD: Johns Hopkins University Center for Social Organization of Schools.

Wheelock, A., & Miao, J. (2005, March). The ninth-grade bottleneck. *The School Administrator.* [Electronic version] Available at http://www.aasa.org/publications/saarticledetail.cfm?ItemNumber=988

White, M. A., & Duker, J. (1973). Models of schooling and models of evaluation. *Teachers College Record, 74*(3), 293–308.

Wigfield, A. (1994). Expectancy-value theory of achievement motivation: A developmental perspective. *Educational Psychology Review, 6,* 49–78.

Wigfield, A., & Eccles, J. S. (1992). The development of achievement task values: A theoretical analysis. *Developmental Review, 12,* 265–310.

William and Flora Hewlett Foundation. (2010, October). *Education program strategic plan.* Menlo Park, CA: Author.

Wilson, T. D., & Linville, P. W. (1982). Improving the academic performance of college freshmen: Attribution therapy revisited. *Journal of Personality and Social Psychology, 42,* 367–376.

Wilson, T. D., & Linville, P. W. (1985). Improving the performance of college freshmen with attributional techniques. *Journal of Personality and Social Psychology, 49,* 287–293.

Wolfe, B. L., & Haveman, R. H. (2002, June). Social and non-market benefits from education in an advanced economy. Paper presented at the Conference Series 47, Education in the 21st Century: Meeting the Challenges of a Changing World, Federal Reserve Bank of Boston, Boston, MA.

Wood, O. A. (1920, January). A failure class in algebra. *The School Review, 28*(1), 41–49.

Wrinkle, W. L. (1935). School marks—why what and how? *Educational Administration and Supervision, 21,* 218–225.

Yang, K. (2004). Southeast Asian American children: Not the "model minority." *The Future of Children, 14*(2), 127–133.

Yeager, D. S., & Walton, G. M. (2011). Social-psychological interventions in education: They're not magic. *Review of Educational Research, 81*(2), 267–301.

Young, M. (1958/1994). *The rise of the meritocracy.* New Brunswick, NJ: Transaction.

Index

About the Author

Camille A. Farrington is a research associate (assistant professor) at The University of Chicago, School of Social Service Administration and the Consortium on Chicago School Research. Her research focuses on how school and classroom programs, policies, and practices shape students' experiences, behaviors, and performance in school, particularly in the context of racially and socioeconomically stratified urban environments. She is an expert on classroom instruction and assessment, academic rigor, academic failure, and psycho-social factors in academic performance. She is lead author of *Teaching Adolescents to Become Learners: The Role of Noncognitive Factors in Shaping School Performance–A Critical Literature Review* (2012) and *A New Model of Student Assessment for the 21st Century* (2008).

Prior to joining The University of Chicago, Dr. Farrington served for 3 years on the faculty at the College of Education, University of Washington, where she taught doctoral courses in educational leadership and policy studies. She is a National Board Certified teacher with 15 years' experience teaching in public high schools in California, Wisconsin, and Illinois. Dr. Farrington received a B.A. from the University of California at Santa Cruz, teacher certification from Mills College, and a Ph.D. in Policy Studies in Urban Education from the University of Illinois at Chicago. She lives in Chicago with her husband, dog, and cat, and is thankful every day that her two daughters somehow survived high school and have moved on to college.